Simply Beautiful Beads

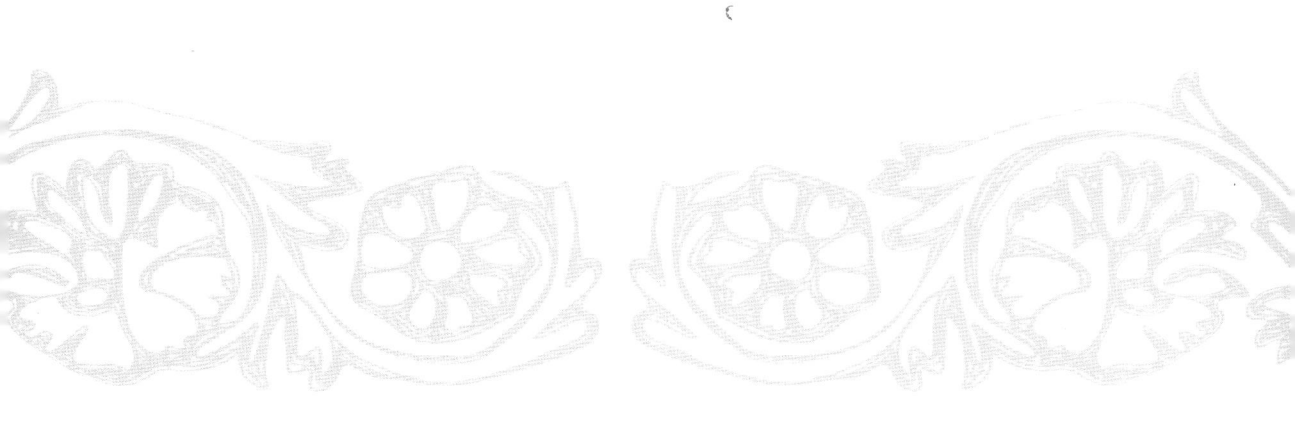

By *Elizabeth Townes*

Copyright © 2015 by BeadJeweled, Inc. All Rights Reserved.

No part of this publication may be reproduced, stored in a retrieval system or transmitted in any form or by any means, electronic, mechanical, photocopying, recording, scanning or otherwise, except as permitted under Sections 107 or 108 of the 1976 United States Copyright Act, without BeadJeweled, Inc. prior written permission. To obtain permission, please call or write to the company using the information below. There may be additional fees depending upon your usage.

Published By:
BeadJeweled, Inc.
2701 W. Busch Blvd. #211
Tampa, FL 33618
Phone (813) 930-6081
Fax (813) 930-6392
www.beadjeweledinc.com

ISBN-13: 978-1500694210

ISBN-10: 1500694215

Acknowledgements

The very first beadweaving class that I taught took place in 2004 when I began teaching at local bead shops in the Tampa Bay area. Since that time, I started teaching at national shows in 2006 and have continued up through the present. Many of the projects presented in this book are classes that I have taught over the last ten years at these national shows. I understand that many wonderful beaders cannot afford to attend the shows and so I have compiled this book to allow everyone the opportunity to create these wonderful classes in the comfort of their own homes.

Through my experience in teaching beadwork, I have learned that people learn in many different ways. Some people are visual (they rely on the charts and graphs) and others are verbal (they rely on the word descriptions) and some people just need a live voice to walk them through it. I have included in this book projects for various levels of beaders, from beginner to advanced. I am always available to answer any questions and guide people. I can be contacted through my email info@beadjeweledinc.com

I would like to thank the many beaders who have taken my classes and in the process often helped me to refine my instructions. Also I would like to thank my patterns testers: Darla Deaton, Pam Hunt and Karie Hieb. These women have waded through the early drafts and helped me with both the visual and the word descriptions. Thanks to them the patterns are far better than I could ever produce by myself.

Also I would like to thank my very talented daughter, Chelsea Townes, who is the artist and graphic designer behind this book. She takes my rudimentary drawings and makes them look nice, designs the page layouts in the book, and keeps with the overall theme that we have chosen for the book. She also takes care of all the photography of the pieces, and I have to say from my own experience that photographing jewelry is a really tough chore. We love sparkle, but often the sparkle is just too much for the camera lens so that creates a challenge.

My Husband, Chuck Cancelliere, also deserves a big thank you. He takes care of the day to day things in our lives so that I can create new beadwork and keep growing my abilities in this ever changing art.

Finally I would like to thank all of my customers who have purchased my books over the last several years. If it were not for your continued support of my efforts, this book would not have some into existence. May you continue to bead happy, healthy and creatively.

Table of Contents

- Encrusted Jewels — pg 08
- Crystal Rondell Pendant — pg 12
- Sapphire Snowflake — pg 15
- Victorian Choker — pg 18
- Cappucino Cascade — pg 23
- Crystal Icicles — pg 26
- Golder Pearl Cuff — pg 29
- Multi-cube Bracelet — pg 32
- Woven Elegance — pg 36
- Crystal Braided Bracelet — pg 39
- Ocean Wave Bracelet — pg 42
- Braided Ndebele Cuff — pg 45
- Russian Leaf Earrings — pg 48
- Framed Peyote Earrings — pg 52
- Winter Snowflake Earrings — pg 55
- Twisted Ribbon Necklace — pg 58
- Fun With Faux Pearls — pg 60
- Peyote Spiral Necklace — pg 62
- La Cote D'Azure — pg 64
- Resources Section — pg 70

Encrusted Jewels Bracelet

Supplies:

- Delica beads (color one) ≈ 10 g
- Delica beads (color two) ≈ 8 g
- Nymo Thread size D
- Beading needles size 12
- Charlottes ≈ 3-4g
- 7-8 tab shaped gemstones
- 50-60 2 to 3 mm gemstones
- 15° seed beads

Weave a stunning bracelet using delicas, odd-count peyote, brick stitch and embellishments.

Nº 8

Stitch the Base

String on 13 delica beads. This will make up the first two rows of the peyote stitch. For row three, pick up 1 bead, go through the second bead previously strung. Pick up a one bead and skip the next bead, going through the next bead to the end of the row.

You are stitching in odd count peyote. See the resource section for odd count peyote instructions.

Stitch in odd count peyote until the band just meets around your wrist. (You may have to adjust the length after you have attached all the medallions).

The ends of the peyote band are finished according to the following diagrams. Because of the way the bracelet is constructed, it is advisable to wait until the medallions are in place to finish the ends.

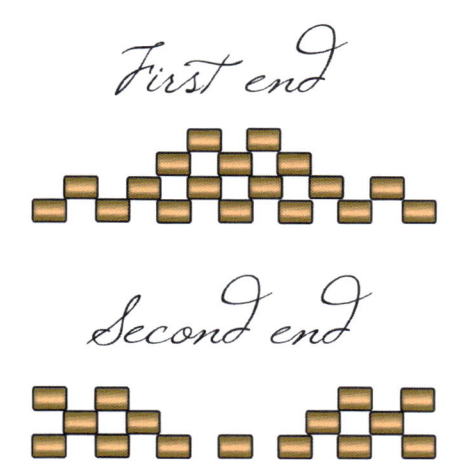

First end

Second end

When the ends are completed they will fit together like two puzzle pieces.

Stitch the Medallion

The medallions are made using Color 2 of the delicas and are stitched in brick stitch. Make a 3-bead ladder, 10 stacks wide. Work in decreasing brick stitch until 5 beads remain. Weave the thread back through to the opposite end. Work in decreasing brick stitch until 5 beads remain. See page resources section for ladder and brick stitch instructions.

Start with three bead ladder.

Each end of the medallion is stitched in decreasing brick stitch after starting with the center ladder rows.

Encrust the Jewels

Center one of the tab shaped gemstones on the medallion. Stitch the tab bead down securely to the medallion by passing the thread through the bead a couple of times. With the thread exiting the medallion by the hole to the tab bead, string on a sufficient number of charlottes to completely encircle the tab bead. Tack the charlottes down to the medallion every three to four beads.

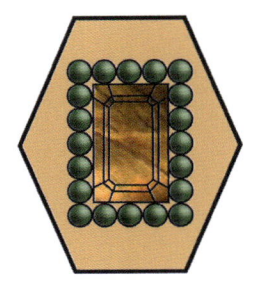

Assembling the bracelet

Begin at one end of the peyote band. Position the medallion so that the edge of the medallion is even with the edge of peyote band. Attach the sides of the medallion to the band by stitching through one bead in the medallion and one bead in the band. You will see that the diagonal lines of the peyote band will line up with the diagonal edges of the medallions. Do not stitch the ends down. The ends will be treated when the embellishment is added to the sides of the band.

Next, attach a row of the small gemstone beads right next to the medallion, but in a straight line. String on a gemstone bead, then a charlotte, then go back through the gemstone bead and into the base. Try to evenly space the beads. See Diagram

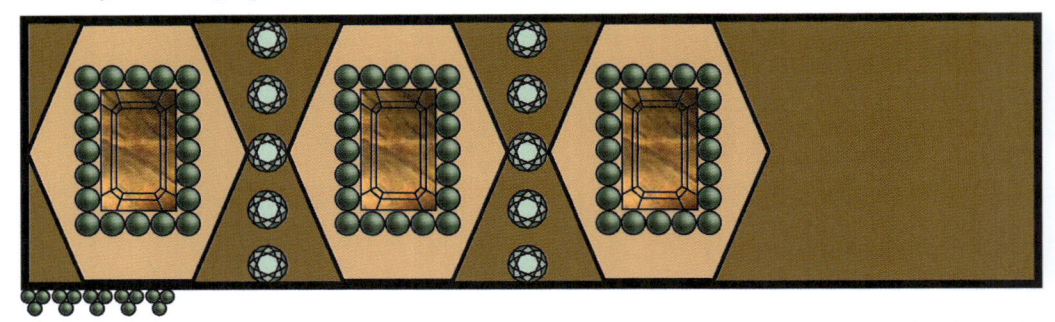

Embellish the sides of the band using a three bead picot stitch with size 15° seed bead. Place the needle through the thread loop on the edge of the band, pick up three beads and go through the next loop on the edge of the band in a whipstitch motion.

When you get to the medallions, go through both the thread loop on the edge of the band and the thread loop on the edge of the medallion, and then add the three beads. This covers the thread loops on the ends of the medallions.

Nº 10

Stitch the Closure Loops

Make two small loops of seed beads on the indented ends of the bracelet. These loops will fit right over the little tabs extending on the other end of the bracelet. Stitch a gemstone bead on each little tab and make sure the loops are large enough to fit over the gemstones. You may want to use elastic thread so they will fit more easily over the gemstones. Stitch three gemstone beads on the other end of the bracelet in the center section.

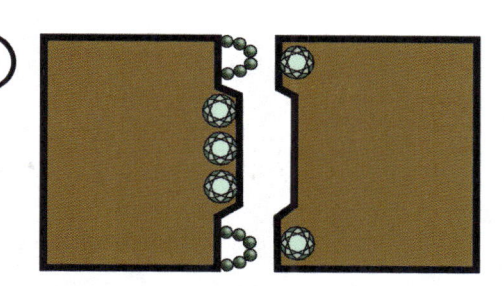

When the loops are placed over the gemstone beads, the effect will be a continuous bracelet with no clasp

Nº11

Crystal Rondelle Pendant

Supplies:

- 1 - 8mm round crystal
- 8 - 6mm round crystals
- 8 - 6mm rhinestone rondelles
- Size 13 charlottes ≈1g
- Beading needles size 12
- Beading Thread

This sparkling pendant is made from Swarovski crystals and sparkling rhinestone rondelles for maximum bling.

Nº12

Construct the Core

The center of the pendant is made using the 8mm round crystal. Thread the needle with about a yard and a half of thread, stretched and conditioned. Thread the 8mm crystal on and tie a knot to secure the thread on the Crystal. Pick up enough charlottes to go half way around the crystal. In the sample we used size 13 charlottes and it took 12 beads. Pass the needle back through the crystal again and string on enough seed beads to complete the other side. Pass the needle back through the crystal once again.

①

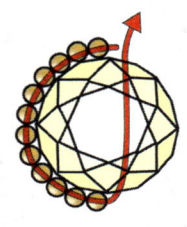

Repeat for the other side, (*See Figure 2.*)

②

Add the Rondelles

Pass the needle through one of the seed beads. Pick up a rondelle and brick stitch the rondelle to the seed bead ring. Pass back through the rondelle and pick up a 6mm crystal and another rondelle. Repeat the step making a brick stitch to add the rondelle, passing back through the rondelle and picking up another crystal and rondelle. The stitch is a variation of a brick stitch so you are actually passing the needle under the thread between the charlottes.

③

Continue in the same manner until you have added eight rondelles and eight crystals. Make sure that you evenly space the rondelles around the 8mm crystal. For example, if you used 24 charlottes to circle the 8 mm crystal, divide that number by eight. The result is 3 so you would skip three charlottes each time so that the eight rondelles are evenly spaced.

Nº 13

Attach the Bail

Pick up twelve seed beads to form a loop at the top to attach the bail. The thread should be exiting a rondelle and going back through the same rondelle to make the loop. Attach the pendant bail to the loop of seed beads. Thread a fine gold chain through the bail and your pendant is ready to wear. If you prefer to make a bail using the charlottes the instructions follow:

Making the Bail

Make a ladder with two beads. String two beads on the needle and go back through the beads again. Arrange the beads so that they are sitting side by side.

(4)

Begin increasing brick stitch by picking up two beads, passing the needle under the threads connecting the previous two beads in the ladder and back up through the second bead added.

(5)

Complete the row by picking up one seed bead, passing down through the bead in the ladder row, catch the thread connecting the two beads in the ladder and pass the needle back up through the bead in the ladder row and the last bead added in the row.

(6)

Continue working in increasing brick stitch until you have seven beads in the row.

Then begin decreasing brick stitch. For a decrease in the row, the first stitch will use the thread loop between the second and third beads in the previous row.

(7)

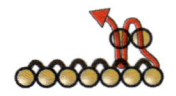

Continue working in increasing brick stitch until you have seven beads in the row.

Pass one end of the bail through the loop on the pendant and connect the two ends of the bail by stitching the two beads in the first row and in the last row together.

Sapphire Snowflake

Supplies:

- 54 4mm bi-cone Swarovski Crystals
- 15° seed beads (small amount)
- Fireline
- Size 10 or 11 needles

Create this fabulous snowflake with circular triangle weave.

Nº 15

Begin the Snow Flake

Thread a needle with about 1-½ yards of thread or Fireline. String on a seed bead, a crystal, a seed bead, a crystal, a seed bead and a crystal. Tie beads into a circle.

1

Weave the thread so that it is exiting one of the crystals. String on a seed bead, a crystal, a seed bead, a crystal and a seed bead. Go back through the crystal that the thread is coming out of. You will be going in a circle.

2

Weave the thread so that it is exiting one of the crystals. String on a seed bead, a crystal, a seed bead, a crystal and a seed bead. Go back through the crystal that the thread is coming out of. You will be going in a circle. Notice that this time you will be going in the opposite direction.

3

Weave the thread so that it is exiting one of the crystals. String on a seed bead, a crystal, a seed bead, a crystal and a seed bead. Go back through the crystal that the thread is coming out of. You will be going in a circle. Notice that this time you will be going in the opposite direction.

4

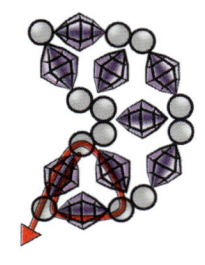

Weave the thread so that it is exiting one of the crystals. String on a seed bead, a crystal, a seed bead, a crystal and a seed bead. Go back through the crystal that the thread is coming out of. You will be going in a circle. Notice that this time you will be going in the opposite direction.

5

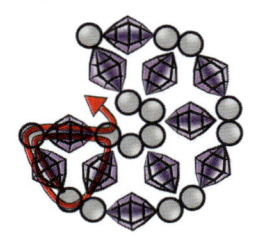

To complete the circle, pick up a seed bead a crystal, and a seed bead. Go through the crystal from the first triangle, pick up another seed bead and go back through the crystal from the last triangle. Weave the thread back to the center of the circle and go through the circle of seeds at the center to pull them tight.

6

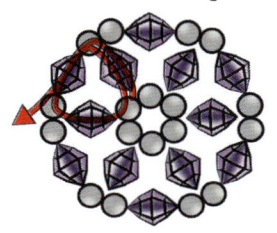

Weave your thread so that it is exiting the circle as shown.

7

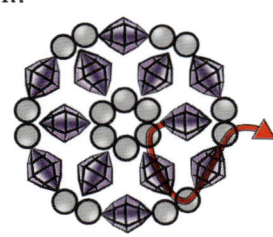

Pick up one seed bead, one crystal, one seed bead, one crystal and one seed bead. Go back through the crystal that the thread is coming out of. Weave back through the beads just added until the thread is coming out of the first crystal added.

8

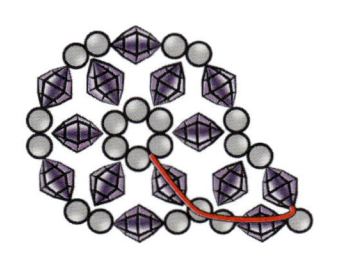

Pick up one seed bead, one crystal, one seed bead, and weave back through the bead added in the last step as shown in the diagram. This will form the point of the icicle. Continue steps 8 and 9 until you have formed 6 points.

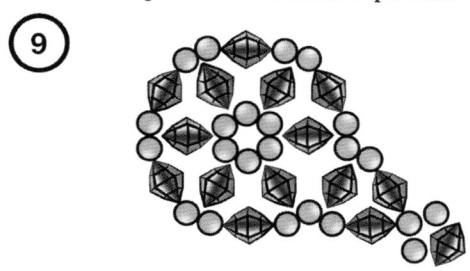

(9)

Now that you have finished the first side of the icicle, we will proceed to the back side. The two sides share the outside beads of the icicle. The shared beads are shaded in this diagram. Begin the second side of the icicle just as you did in steps 1 – 8. In step 9 you will pick up a seed bead, go through the shared bead from the first side of the icicle and then pick up a seed bead, thereby completing step nine by substituting a shared bead for a crystal. Repeat for each of the six points.

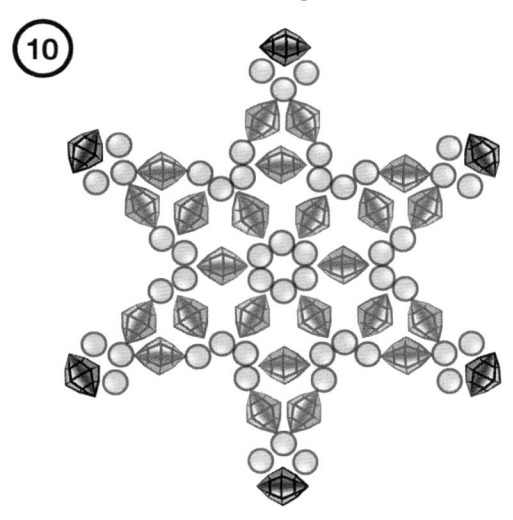

(10)

Add a loop of seed beads in order to create a bail. We used 18 seed beads and went back through them several times to create strength at the stress point.

Victorian Choker

Supplies:

- 250 - 4mm Firepolish
- 11° seed beads ≈ 9g
- 4 lb smoke Fireline
- Beading Needle

Use Firepolish and seed beads to weave this choker with an adjustable closure.

Nº 18

Start the Inner Filigree

Thread a needle with about 1-½ yards of thread or Fireline. String on a seed bead, a crystal, a seed bead, a crystal, a seed bead and a crystal. Tie beads into a circle.

①

Weave the thread so that it is exiting one of the 4mm Firepolish. String on a seed bead, a 4mm Firepolish, a seed bead, a 4mm Firepolish and a seed bead. Go back through the 4mm Firepolish that the thread is coming out of. You will be going in a circle.

②

Weave the thread so that it is exiting one of the 4mm Firepolish. String on a seed bead, a 4mm Firepolish, a seed bead, a 4mm Firepolish and a seed bead. Go back through the 4mm Firepolish that the thread is coming out of. You will be going in a circle. Notice that this time you will be going in the opposite direction.

③

Weave the thread so that it is exiting one of the 4mm Firepolish. String on a seed bead, a 4mm Firepolish, a seed bead, a 4mm Firepolish and a seed bead. Go back through the 4mm Firepolish that the thread is coming out of. You will be going in a circle.

④

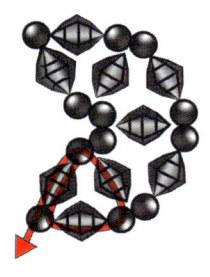

Weave the thread so that it is exiting one of the 4mm Firepolish. String on a seed bead, a 4mm Firepolish, a seed bead, a 4mm Firepolish and a seed bead. Go back through the 4mm Firepolish that the thread is coming out of. You will be going in a circle. Notice that this time you will be going in the opposite direction.

⑤

To complete the circle, pick up a seed bead a 4mm Firepolish, and a seed bead. Go through the 4mm Firepolish from the first triangle, pick up another seed bead and go back through the 4mm Firepolish from the last triangle. Weave the thread back to the center of the circle and go through the six seed beads at the center of the circle to pull them tight.

⑥

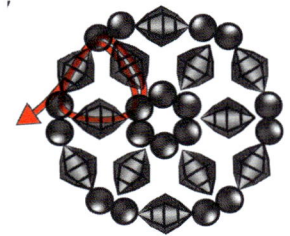

The circles in the choker will share one 4mm Firepolish bead. The next circle you will stitch you will use a shared bead like in this diagram. Weave your thread so that it is exiting the circle as shown below. There are six "spoke" beads in each circle and six outside beads in each circle. When I refer to a "spoke" bead that will be the one that points to the center of the circle.

⑦

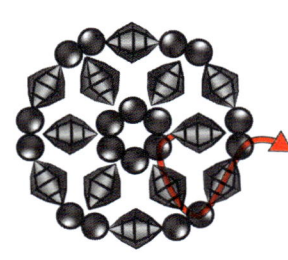

Nº 19

I am not going to draw every thread path now because it is basically the same for each of the circles. Always make sure that your needle is coming out of a "spoke" bead before picking up the beads for the next step.

Pick up one seed bead, one 4mm Firepolish, one seed bead, one 4mm Firepolish and one seed bead. Go back through the 4mm Firepolish that the thread is coming out of. Weave back through the beads just added until the thread is coming out of the "spoke" bead.

(8)

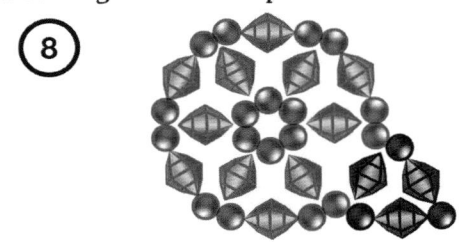

Pick up one seed bead, one 4mm Firepolish, one seed bead, one 4mm Firepolish and one seed bead. Go back through the 4mm Firepolish that the thread is coming out of. Weave back through the beads just added until the thread is coming out of the "spoke" bead.

(9)

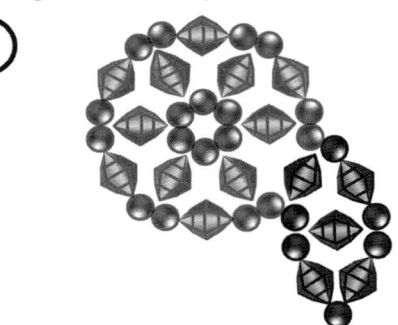

Pick up one seed bead, one 4mm Firepolish, one seed bead, one 4mm Firepolish and one seed bead. Go back through the 4mm Firepolish that the thread is coming out of. Weave back through the beads just added until the thread is coming out of the "spoke" bead.

(10)

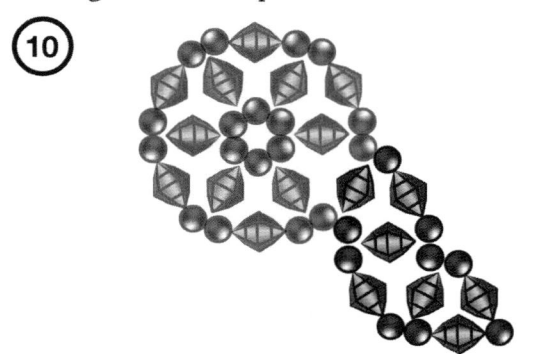

Pick up one seed bead, one 4mm Firepolish, one seed bead, one 4mm Firepolish and one seed bead. Go back through the 4mm Firepolish that the thread is coming out of. Weave back through the beads just added until the thread is coming out of the "spoke" bead.

(11)

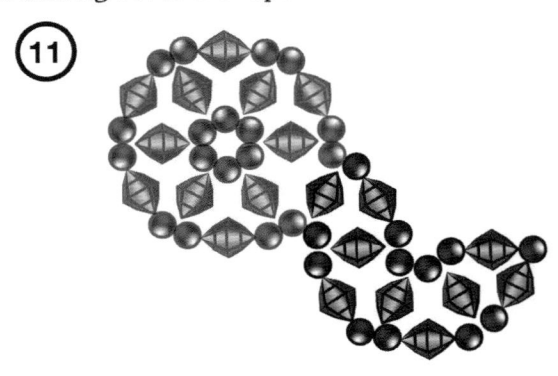

Pick up one seed bead, one 4mm Firepolish, one seed bead, one 4mm Firepolish and one seed bead. Go back through the 4mm Firepolish that the thread is coming out of. Weave back through the beads just added until the thread is coming out of the "spoke" bead.

(12)

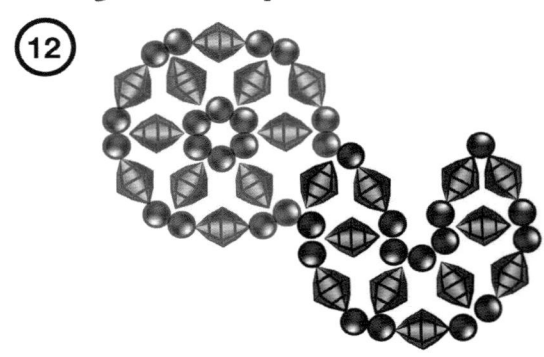

Pick up a seed bead, a 4mm Firepolish and a seed bead and go through the first spoke bead in the circle. Pick up a seed bead and go through the last "spoke" bead in the circle.

(13)

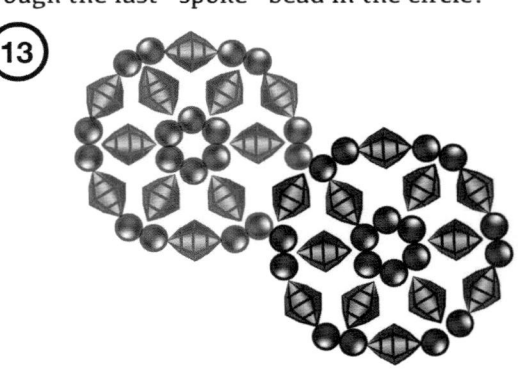

N°20

Work in triangular weave to get the needle exiting on the opposite side of the circle just added as shown in step 7. Repeat steps 7 through 14 until you have 20 circles.

Now we will begin the embellishment. Weave your thread so that you are coming out of the four seed beads that lie between the two circles.

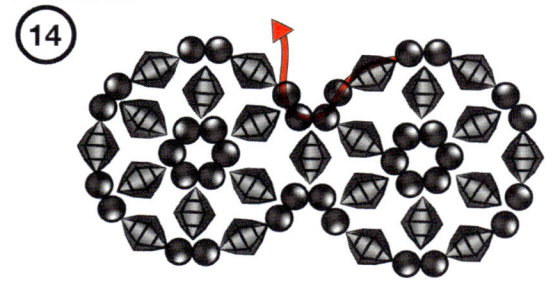

⑭

Begin the Loops

Pick up 8 seed beads, go back through the 7th bead added, pick up three more seed beads, go through the 3rd bead added, pick up 2 more seed beads and go back through the original four seed beads that lie between the two circles.

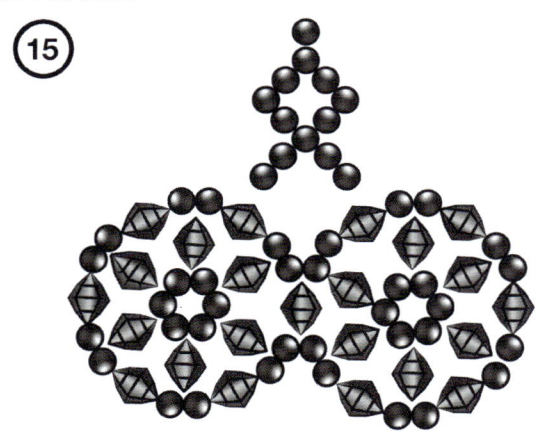

⑮

Weave the thread back through the beads skipping numbers 5, 7 and 8, and 10. Weave back through the original four beads and pull the tension very tight to make the beads pop out and form corners.

Weave through the circles in triangular weave to the next intersection between the circles and repeat steps 16 and 17 until all the intersections of the circles have been completed on one side of the choker.

For the next pass, working on the same side of the choker, weave your thread so that it is exiting the two beads on the top of a circle. Add two beads, weave through the beads added in step 16 as shown in the diagram, add two more seed beads and weave through the two beads at the top of the next circle. Continue across the entire top of the choker. Note: this step is going to make your necklace curve into a semi-circle.

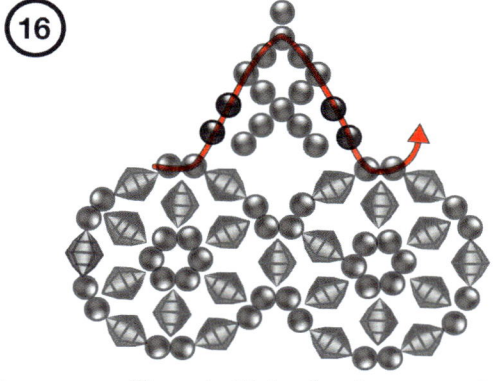

⑯

Now we will embellish the bottom of the choker. Weave your thread so that it is exiting the four seed beads that lie between the circles.

String on 10 seed beads, go back through the ninth seed bead, string on 5 seed beads, and go back through the third bead strung. Pick up 2 seed beads and go then back into the four seed beads. Weave the thread back through the beads skipping numbers 6, 9 and 10, and 13. Weave back through the original four beads and pull the tension very tight to make the beads pop out and form corners.

Weave through to the next four seed beads in between the circles and repeat step 20.

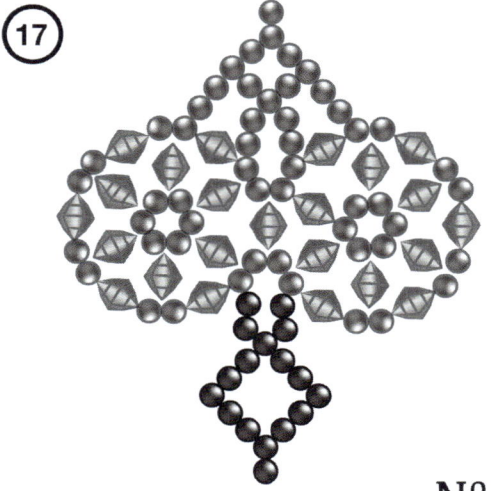

⑰

Nº21

For the return pass on the bottom side, with the thread exiting between the two beads at the bottom of a circle, string on 10 seed beads, pass through the point bead from the previous step, string on 10 more seed beads and pass the thread around the threads between the two seed beads at the bottom of the next circle.

(18)

Go back through the last three beads from the previous step and string on 7 seed beads. Pass through the point bead from the previous step, string on 10 more seed beads and pass the thread around the threads between the two seed beads at the bottom of the next circle.

(19)

Making the Clasp

With the needle exiting on one side of the 4mm Firepolish bead on one of the ends, string on 3 seed beads, *1 Firepolish, 6 seed beads, and repeat from the * six more times. String on 1 Firepolish and 1 seed bead. Pass the needle back though the Firepolish only. At this point you will be heading back in the opposite direction. Then string on 6 seed beads between each Firepolish and pass the needle through the Firepolish previously strung. After the last Firepolish, string on 3 seed beads and go back through the 4mm Firepolish bead in the opposite direction. Follow the same thread path 2 more times to reinforce. Weave the Fireline in and knot a few times. Repeat on the other end of the necklace.

The necklace fastens by passing one of the ends through a loop in the other end of the necklace. The loop you choose will be the one that adjusts the size to your neck and the placement of the necklace as you desire.

Cappuccino Cascade

Supplies:

- white rice pearls ≈ 4 strands
- peach rice pearls ≈ 2 strands
- white potato pearls ≈ 1 strands
- bronze potato pearls ≈ 1 strands
- peach potato pearls ≈ 1 strands
- size 15 seed beads ≈ 3g
- lobster claw clasp
- beading needles size 12
- size 8 seed beads ≈ 6g
- 2 jump rings
- Nymo thread size D

In the style of Marian Haskell, this necklace is a waterfall of coffee colored pearls.

N°23

Create the Slide

The slide is made using peyote stitch with rice pearls and seed beads.

String on alternating size 15 seed beads and rice pearls beads until you have 10 rice pearls ending with a size 15 seed bead.

Pick up one size 15, a rice pearl, one size 15 and go through the rice pearl in the previous row. Continue peyote across the row using the same stitch.

Repeat the row above until you have 16 rows of peyote (you can tell that you have 16 when there are 8 pearls on each end.) Roll the peyote strip up and "zip" it together to form a tube.

Add the Cascade

The cascade is made from fringe created from different colors and sizes of pearls.

The first row is the shortest row. With your needle coming out of one of the end pearls on the slide, facing the center of the slide, string on the beads according to the chart below. You will use the same row of pearls in the slide to attach two rows of fringe. Then attach rows three and four to the peyote row directly behind the row with the first two rows of fringe. Each fringe piece will hang underneath a rice pearl. Your thread will be coming out of a size 15 on one side of the rice pearl and after making the fringe the thread will pass through the 15 on the other side of the pearl.

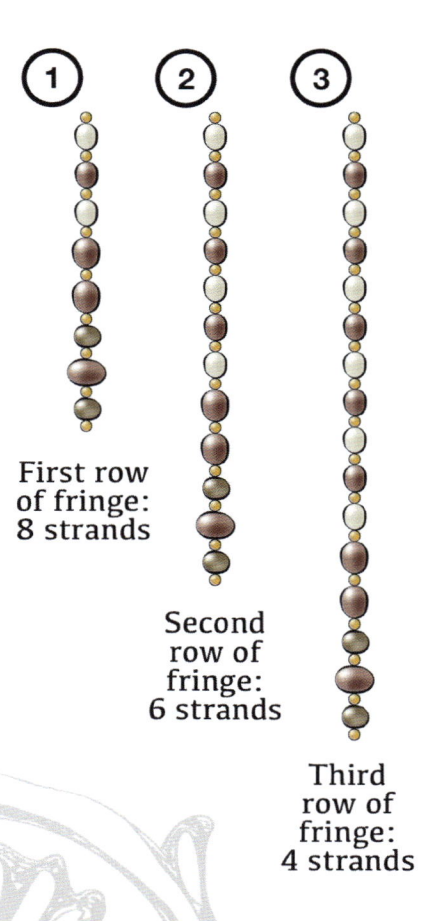

1 First row of fringe: 8 strands

2 Second row of fringe: 6 strands

3 Third row of fringe: 4 strands

4 Fourth row of fringe: 8 strands

N°24

Stitch the Rope

The spiral rope is made with a core of size 8 seed beads, and he spirals consist of a size 15, a pearl, and a size 15. Begin stringing on four size 8 seed beads, one 15, one pearl and one 15. Go back through all four size 8 seed beads in the same direction as you went when you originally strung them on.

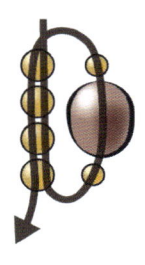

(5)

Next pick up one size 8, one size 15, one pearl, one size 15 and go back through the last three of the previously strung beads. See diagram. Be sure to push the spirals to the same side each time. If you do not do this, then the spiral will not work properly. Stitch the spiral long enough for one side of the neck strap. For the part where the slide will be use 5 size 15s for the spiral and not the pearls. Put the slide onto the spiral before continuing with the second side.

(6)

Attach a clasp to each end of the spiral rope when it is the desired length.

Crystal Icicles Necklace

Supplies:

- 11° delicas ≈ 10g
  (*silver lined Crystal*)
- 15 4 mm Swarovski bi-cone crystals
- Small Magnetic clasp
- Nymo Thread size D white
- Beading needles size 12
- Softflex beading wire
- Crimp beads

Use brick stitch to create a sparkler for the holidays.

N°26

Stitch the Center Piece

Thread your needle with about 2 ½ yards of thread. Stretch the thread and use some Thread Heaven if desired. Do not use wax as it tends to discolor the beads and thread and takes away from the sparkling impact of the necklace.

Begin by making a ladder 6 beads long. Work in brick stitch upwards to the top of the piece, then weave the thread back through and continue stitching downward following diagram 2.

My preference is to complete one diamond shape and then begin adding beads to the sides to create the next diamond shape. You may have a better method of working but this one works for me. Diagram 2 is color-graded so that you can clearly see each of the diamond shapes.

Add the Crystal

When you reach the point of the diamond, instead of adding a seed bead, use a 4 mm crystal with a seed bead. Go back through the crystal to attach it to the work.

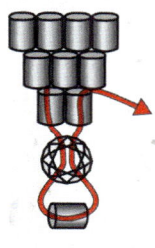

N°27

Stitch the Side Pieces

Using diagram 2, stitch 4 two-diamond pieces, 4 single-diamond pieces with crystals and 2 single-diamond pieces with no crystals. For the single diamond use only the first diamond portion of the chart. For the two-diamond pieces use the first and second (*light grey diamond*) portion of the chart. The center diamond uses all of the chart.

String the Necklace

Using flexible beading wire, string the necklace as follows:

    Seed beads
Single diamond piece no crystals
10 seed beads
Single diamond piece with crystals
10 seed beads
Single diamond piece with crystals
10 seed beads
Double diamond piece
12 seed beads
Double diamond piece
12 seed beads
Center triple diamond piece.

Reverse for the second half of the necklace.

Attach the Clasp

String on a crimp bead, one-half of the clasp and thread the wire back through the crimp bead. Crimp securely.

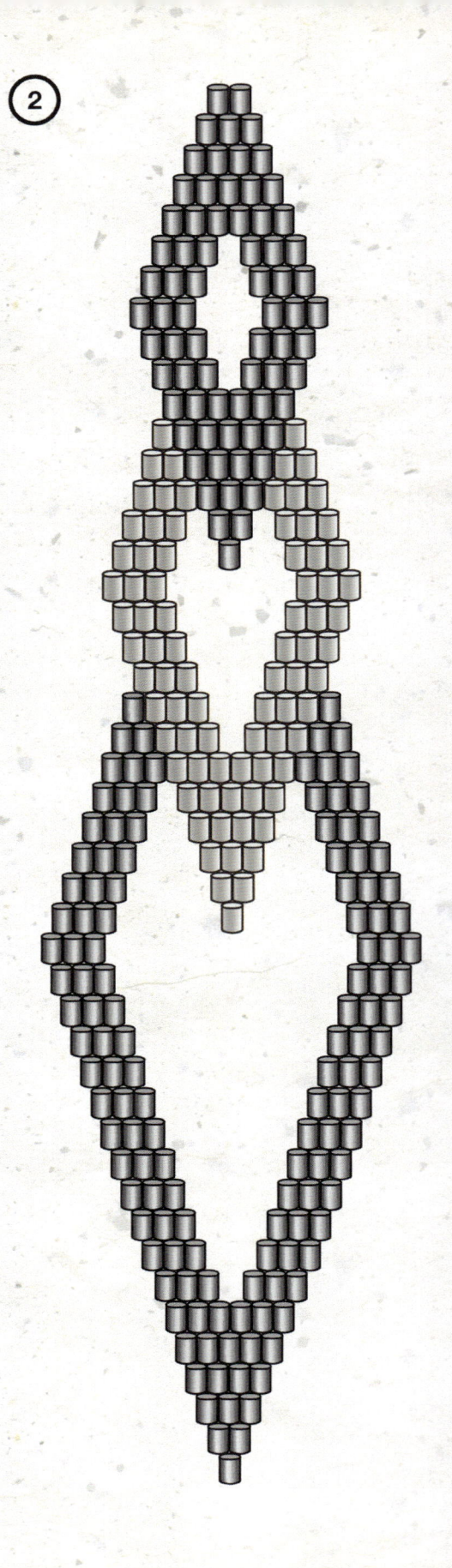

Golden Pearl Cuff

Supplies:

- 2 strands of pearls (5-6mm)
- 8° seed beads to match contrast colored pearls ≈ 2g
- 1 strand pearls in contrast color (*or sub 6mm bi-cone crystals*)
- French Wire or thread protectors
- Magnetic clasp
- Nymo Thread or Fireline (*Particularly if using crystals*)
- Magnifiers if needed
- Beading needles size 12

This pearl cuff forms a curve as you embellish the basic right angle weave base.

N°29

Stitch the Base

Stitch the base in Right Angle Weave (RAW) and then add embellishment on top of the base. See the resources page for basics on RAW.

String on 4 pearls and go back through all four pearls in the same direction. Tie a knot to secure the threads.

①

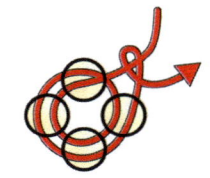

Pick up three pearls and go back through the last pearl added. Go through the bead from the previous set and the first two beads just added. The new beads are outlined in black.

②

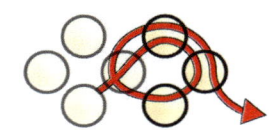

Pick up three pearls and go back through the last pearl added. Go through the bead from the previous set and the first two beads just added. The new beads are outlined in black.

③

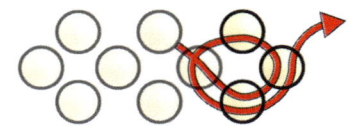

Continue the pattern until the length is sufficient to go around the wrist with some extra room. The length should be a bit longer than you need since it will become shorter as the embellishment is added. Make sure you have an even number of sets of RAW. Don't worry, though – you can adjust the length before the clasp is finished. Continue adding a second row of RAW by adding three beads for the first step and then two beads for each section after that.

④

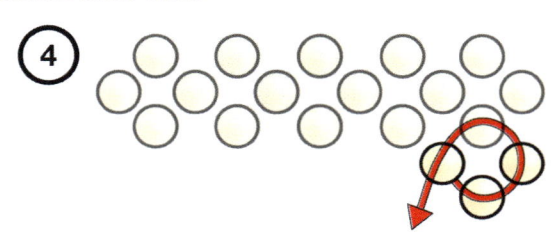

Your bracelet base will look like this when you complete the second row of RAW.

⑤

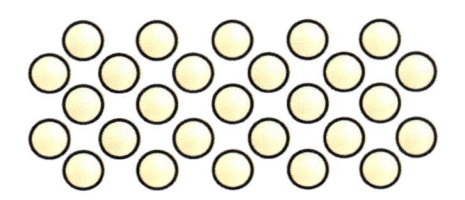

Add gold pearls down the center of the bracelet by stitching through the center row of white pearls. The bracelet will begin to curve into a circle.

⑥

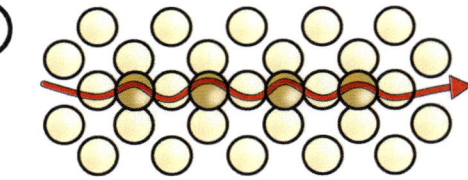

Add one size 8 seed bead between each of the pearls on the edge of the bracelet. This step will begin to shape the bracelet which will eventually take on a dome shape.

⑦

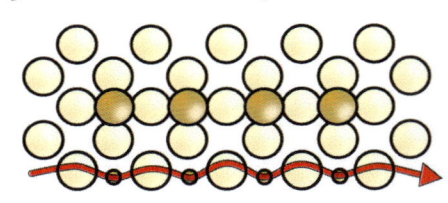

When you get to the end of the bracelet add one half of the clasp (use either French wire or thread protectors to prevent the clasp from cutting the thread) and continue to add a size 8 bead between each of the pearls on the other side of the bracelet.

⑧

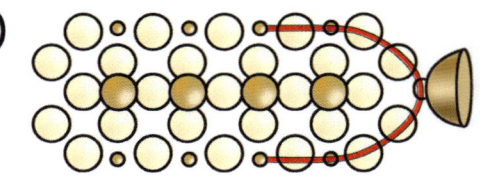

Check the length of the bracelet before adding the other side of the clasp. If you need to lengthen the bracelet, add more RAW sets of the white pearls and embellish as before. When the length is good, add the other side of the clasp to the other end of the bracelet. Again I would suggest using either French wire or thread protectors.

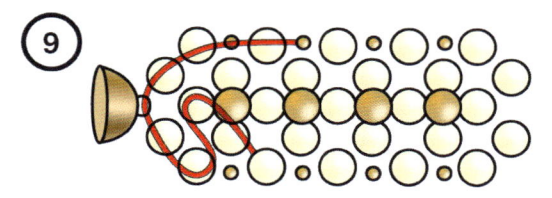

Embellish the top of the cuff with size 8 seed beads. With your thread exiting the first gold pearl, pick up five beads and go diagonally to the size 8 seed bead on the edge of the bracelet following the diagram below.

Repeat the embellishment on the other side of he bracelet, forming the diamond shapes as shown below.

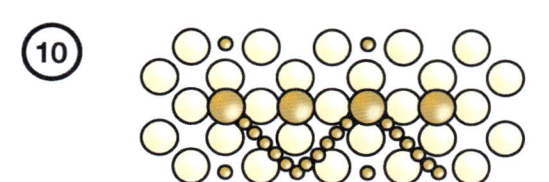

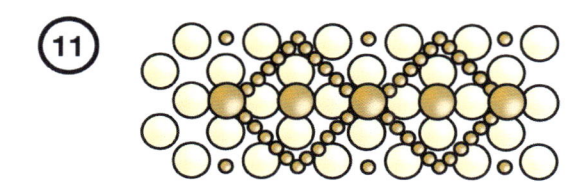

Nº31

Multi Cube Bracelet

Supplies:

- Delica beads
- 4mm cube beads
- Basketweave crimp ends
- E 5000 glue
- Nymo Thread size D to match beads as closely as possible
- Beading needles size 11

Weave a stunning colored cube bracelet using Delicas and cubes.

N° 32

Stitch a Ladder

To make the ladder, string on four beads and go back through the first two beads strung. Add two beads and pass the needle back through the previous two bead stack, then through the two beads just added. See Diagram 1.

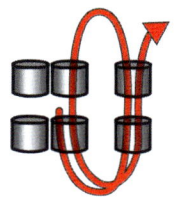

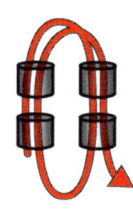

①

②

Continue this until you have a ladder that is 16 stacks long. See the Resource Section for basics on the ladder stitch.

Join the ladder into a circle and flatten the ladder strip so that you have 8 stacks on each side. Stitch one row of herringbone all the way around the stacks so that you have three rows.

③

Begin Stitching the "Fingers"

At this point you will begin stitching fingers first using four beads from the base rows.

I refer to this step as stitching fingers because each narrow strip is stitched and then the "fingers" and woven together using a zig zag through the cubes.

For the first "finger", you will use four beads, two from the front and two from the back of the base rows. See Figure 3.

Nº 33

With the thread exiting the first bead in the herringbone stack, pick up a cube bead and two delica beads. Snug the cube down against the previous herringbone rows and pass the needle back down through the cube and into the second bead of the previous herringbone stitch (*See diagram 4.*) See the resource section for the basics on herringbone stitch.

In essence, you are continuing the herringbone stitch but you have placed a cube in the middle of the herringbone stitch. Bring the needle up through the first bead in the back of the herringbone stack and pass the needle back up through the cube bead. Pick up two delica beads, pass the needle back down through the cube and through the second bead in the back herringbone stack. Pass the needle through the first bead in the front stack and back up through the cube and through the first delica bead sitting on top of the cube, continuing the herringbone stitch just as if the cube wasn't even there.

You will be adding cubes between each set of herringbone beads for the entire length of the first "finger." You may wish to establish a pattern for the different colors of cubes. The "finger should be long enough to go around your wrist minus the width of the clasp. On the end of the "finger" stitch three rows of herringbone so that it matches the beginning of the "finger."

In between the "fingers" you will use one delica from the base row front and one from the base row back. Stitch a two bead herringbone strip. You will need four rows of herringbone for each cube in the "finger."

This strip of herringbone will go up against the side of the "finger" so that one bead shows in the front and one bead shows in the back.

Joining the "Fingers"

After you have completed the first finger and a herringbone strip, weave the two together by making a circle stitch to connect to the delicas between the cubes. *(See Diagram 5.)* You will need to do this on the front of the bracelet and on the back of the bracelet.

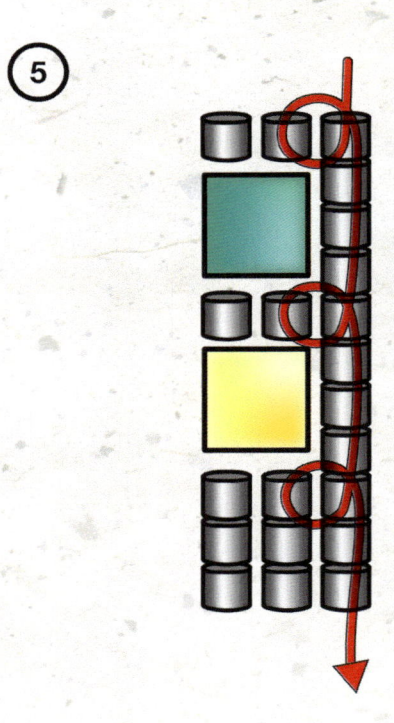

Finishing the End

After all the fingers are stitched, connect the last two herringbone rows by using the circle stitch so that it looks like the two row ladder that you used to begin the bracelet.

Attach the Clasp

Open the crimp end using long nosed pliers so that the end of the bracelet will fit easily into the crimp end. Put a small amount of glue inside the crimp end and place the ends of the bracelet into the crimp end. Let the glue dry for a bit and then using pliers gently squeeze the crimp end so that it tightly hugs the beads. Don't squeeze too tightly or you will break the glass beads inside the clasp. Once the glue has dried, attach the jump rings and the lobster claw clasp. Enjoy wearing your new bracelet.

Nº 35

Woven Elegance Bracelet

Supplies:

- Delica beads ≈10g
- 4 mm cube beads ≈16g
- Basketweave crimp ends ≈25mm
- E 5000 glue
- Nymo Thread size D to match the beads as closely as possible
- Beading Needles Size 12

Weave a basket weave bracelet using delicas and cubes.

Nº 36

Determine the Width of your Bracelet

The width of your bracelet may be dependent upon the width of the clasp that you plan to use. In the case of the example shown here, I used a basketweave crimp end type of clasp and the width of the clasp was the same as seven of the cube beads. This meant that I needed to stitch seven "fingers" to make the bracelet wide enough. Therefore, for each cube width you need, you will need to start a ladder with four ladder sections per cube bead. I used a 28 bead ladder 2 beads high. See the resource section for basics on ladder stitch.

To make the ladder, string on four beads and go back through the first two beads strung. Add two beads and pass the needle back through the previous two bead stack, then through the two beads just added. (*See diagram 1.*)

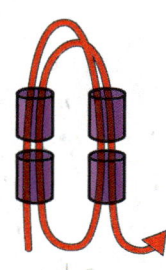

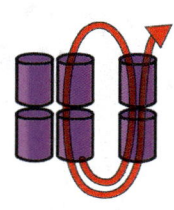

Continue this until you have a ladder that is 28 stacks long (*or whatever you measurement is.*)

Join the ladder into a circle and flatten the ladder strip so that you have 14 stacks on each side. You will be working with four stacks at a time, two in the front and two in the back.

Begin the "Fingers"

I refer to this step as stitching fingers because each narrow strip is stitched and then the "fingers" and woven together using a zig zag through the cubes.

For the first "finger", you will stitch four rows of herringbone using the first two bead stacks in the front and on the back of the ladder strip. (*See diagram 3.*)

After the first four rows are completed, with the thread exiting the first bead in the herringbone stack, pick up a cube bead and two delica beads. Snug the cube down against the previous herringbone rows and pass the needle back down through the cube and into the second bead of the previous herringbone stitch. (*See diagram 4.*) See the resource section for basics on the herringbone stitch.

In essence, you are continuing the herringbone stitch but you have placed a cube in the middle of the herringbone stitch. Bring the needle up through the first bead in the back of the herringbone stack and pass the needle back up through the cube bead. Pick up two delica beads, pass the needle back down through the cube and through the second bead in the back herringbone stack. Pass the needle through the first bead in the front stack and back up through the cube and through the first delica bead sitting on top of the cube, continuing the herringbone stitch just as if the cube wasn't even there.

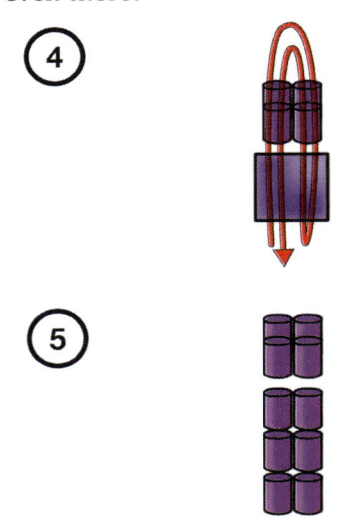

Complete three rows of herringbone (*Including the row made when adding the cube*) and repeat the process of adding the cube bead. You will have three rows of delicas in between each cube.

For "finger" two you will begin with seven rows of herringbone and then add a cube. All even "fingers" will begin with seven rows and all odd "fingers" will begin with four rows.

End the even rows with three rows of herringbone and end the odd "fingers" with six rows of herringbone. Odd rows will have one less cube than the even rows.

Joining the "Fingers"

After you have completed the first two fingers, weave the two "fingers" together by zig-zagging between the cubes in each "finger."

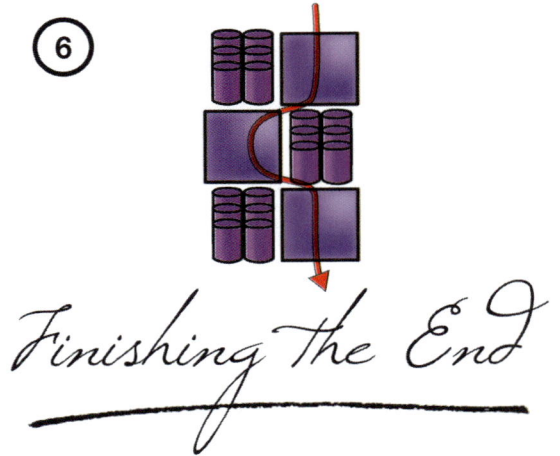

Finishing the End

After all the fingers are stitched, do one complete row of herringbone all the way around all the fingers like you would if you hadn't made each one separately. Then finish with a row of two bead ladder stitch so that the end of the bracelet matches the beginning of the bracelet.

Attach the Clasp

Put a small amount of glue inside the clasp and place the ends of the bracelet into the clasp. Let the glue dry for a bit and then using pliers gently squeeze the clasp so that if tightly hugs the beads. Don't squeeze too tightly or you will break the glass beads inside the clasp.

Crystal Braided Bracelet

Supplies:

- 30 Swarovski round 6mm crystals
- 11° seed beads
- crystal Fireline
- 2 needles size 10 or 11
- 2 thread protectors
- 1 filigree box clasp

Use crystals and seed beads to create a pretty bracelet with a braided edge.

N°39

Begin the Base

Thread two needles (*one on each end*) on a four yard piece of Fireline. String on the thread protector and one half of the clasp. Center the clasp on the Fireline.

Using one needle (*for purposes of illustration we will call this the blue needle*), pick up 3 seed beads, a crystal, three seed beads, a crystal and continue in this pattern until there are 30 crystals on the Fireline.

Using the other needle (*the red one in the illustrations*), pick up three seed beads, and go through the first crystal on the other side. See Diagram. Note that the red needle goes through the crystal in the '*opposite*' direction than the blue needle.

①

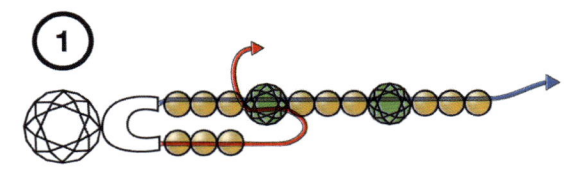

Notice that the needles change positions after going through the crystal.

②

Now place three seed beads on the red needle and go through the next crystal again in the opposite direction as the blue needle. Repeat this step until all the crystals are used.

The thirty crystals will result in a bracelet measuring 8" including the clasp. Each crystal will add or subtract about ¼" from the total length, so you may want to adjust the size of the bracelet before going on to the next step.

Finish the second end in the same manner as the first end. String on 3 seed beads, the thread protector, the other half of the clasp using the blue thread, and then add three more seed beads. Go through the last crystal. Using the red thread, go through the three seed beads, the thread protector and through the three seed beads on the red thread, finally going through the crystal in the opposite direction from the blue thread. See Diagram for the thread path.

③

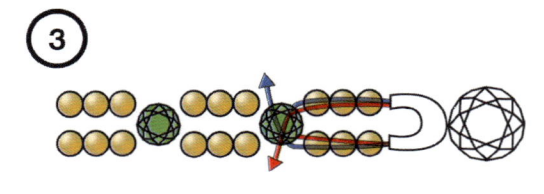

Start the Braid

Now pick up 17 seed beads on the blue needle, go back through the first seed bead added, then back through the crystal, through the next three seed beads and through the next crystal.

Repeat the same with the red needle. Pick up 17 seed beads on the blue needle, go back through the first seed bead added, back through the crystal, through the next three seed beads and through the next crystal.

④

Continue making loops until you reach the next to the last crystal. Now it is time to braid the loops. Pull the second loop through the first loop. Then pull the third loop through the second loop. You may wish to use a crochet hook to help with the task. See the Diagram.

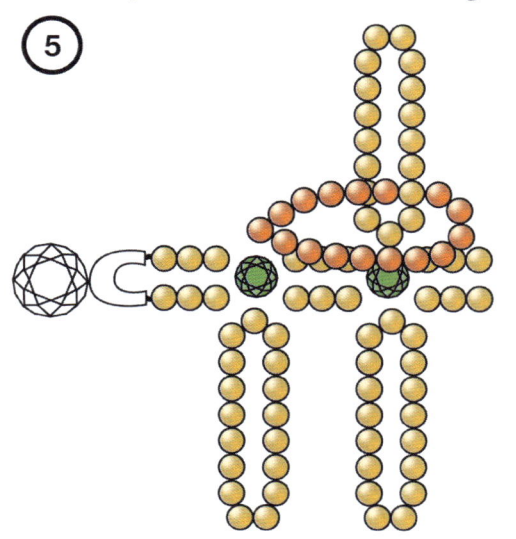

(5)

When the braiding is complete, pass the thread through the last loop, pickup 7 seed beads, pass the needle under the three seed beads leading to the clasp, pick up 6 seed beads and go back through the first seed bead to anchor the braid. Weave through a few beads, tie some half hitch knots and bury the Fireline.

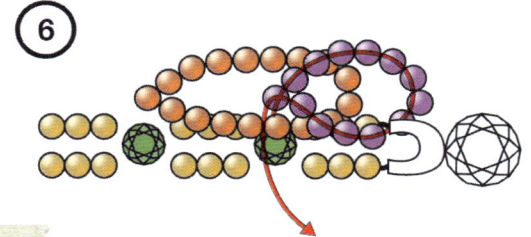

(6)

Nº 41

Ocean Waves Knitted Bracelet

Supplies:

- No. 8 Pearl Cotton (*1 ball*)
- 20 g 11° seed beads
- Big eye needle
- Knitting needles size 0000
- Clasp

Knitting with beads produces a very flexible fabric with a wave pattern.

N° 42

Choosing the Length of Your Bracelet

Thread pearl cotton onto big eye needle. String all size 11 beads onto the pearl cotton. Rewind the cotton making sure that there is sufficient working thread without beads to begin with. You will have to readjust the position of the beads from time to time throughout the knitting process. Helpful hint: Place the ball of pearl cotton in a cup to help control.

The following directions are for a med/large bracelet (*approximately 7 ½ inches*). Since the bracelet is knitted it will stretch to about 8 ½ inches. Skip to Page 4 for directions for a Small/Medium bracelet (*approximately 6 ½ inches, stretch to about 7 ½ inches*).

Medium To Large Bracelet Size

Cast on 12 stitches. When casting on it is helpful to cast on around two knitting needles to ensure that the tension remains loose. Otherwise if the tension is too tight it is difficult to knit the first row.

Rows 1 - 12	knit across
Rows 13 - 18	Slip the first stitch (Sl 1), Knit 1 (K1), Slide one bead (SB1), K2, SB1, K2, SB1, K2, SB1, K2, SB1, K2
Rows 19 - 20	SL1, K1, SB1, K2, SB2, K2, SB1, K2, SB2, K2, SB1, K2
Rows 21 - 22	SL1, K1, SB1, K2, SB3, K2, SB1, K2, SB3, K2, SB1, K2
Rows 23 - 24	SL1, K1, SB1, K2, SB4, K2, SB1, K2, SB4, K2, SB1, K2
Rows 25 - 26	SL1, K1, SB1, K2, SB5, K2, SB1, K2, SB5, K2, SB1, K2
Rows 27 - 28	SL1, K1, SB1, K2, SB6, K2, SB1, K2, SB6, K2, SB1, K2
Rows 29 - 30	SL1, K1, SB1, K2, SB7, K2, SB1, K2, SB7, K2, SB1, K2
Rows 31 - 32**	SL1, K1, SB2, K2, SB6, K2, SB2, K2, SB6, K2, SB2, K2
Rows 33 - 34	SL1, K1, SB3, K2, SB5, K2, SB3, K2, SB5, K2, SB3, K2
Rows 35 - 36	SL1, K1, SB4, K2, SB4, K2, SB4, K2, SB4, K2, SB4, K2
Rows 37 - 38	SL1, K1, SB5, K2, SB3, K2, SB5, K2, SB3, K2, SB5, K2
Rows 39 - 40	SL1, K1, SB6, K2, SB2, K2, SB6, K2, SB2, K2, SB6, K2
Rows 41 - 42	SL1, K1, SB7, K2, SB1, K2, SB7, K2, SB1, K2, SB7, K2
Rows 43 - 44	SL1, K1, SB6, K2, SB2, K2, SB6, K2, SB2, K2, SB6, K2
Rows 45 - 46	SL1, K1, SB5, K2, SB3, K2, SB5, K2, SB3, K2, SB5, K2
Rows 47 - 48	SL1, K1, SB4, K2, SB4, K2, SB4, K2, SB4, K2, SB4, K2
Rows 49 - 50	SL1, K1, SB3, K2, SB5, K2, SB3, K2, SB5, K2, SB3, K2
Rows 51 - 52	SL1, K1, SB2, K2, SB6, K2, SB2, K2, SB6, K2, SB2, K2
Rows 53 - 54	SL1, K1, SB1, K2, SB7, K2, SB1, K2, SB7, K2, SB1, K2**

Repeat pattern from ** to ** three times to complete Rows 55 – 126

Rows 127 - 128	SL1, K1, SB1, K2, SB6, K2, SB1, K2, SB6, K2, SB1, K2
Rows 129 - 130	SL1, K1, SB1, K2, SB5, K2, SB1, K2, SB5, K2, SB1, K2
Rows 131 - 132	SL1, K1, SB1, K2, SB4, K2, SB1, K2, SB4, K2, SB1, K2
Rows 133 - 134	SL1, K1, SB1, K2, SB3, K2, SB1, K2, SB3, K2, SB1, K2
Rows 135 - 136	SL1, K1, SB1, K2, SB2, K2, SB1, K2, SB2, K2, SB1, K2
Rows 137 - 142	SL1, K1, SB1, K2, SB1, K2, SB1, K2, SB1, K2, SB1, K2
Rows 143 - 154	Knit across and bind off

N°43

Small to Medium Bracelet Size

Cast on 12 stitches. When casting on it is helpful to cast on around two knitting needles to ensure that the tension remains loose. Otherwise if the tension is too tight it is difficult to knit the first row.

Rows 1 - 12	Knit across
Rows 13 - 18	Slip the first stitch (Sl 1), Knit 1 (K1), Slide one bead (SB1), K2, SB1, K2, SB1, K2, SB1, K2, SB1, K2
Rows 19 - 20	SL1, K1, SB1, K2, SB2, K2, SB1, K2, SB2, K2, SB1, K2
Rows 21 - 22	SL1, K1, SB1, K2, SB3, K2, SB1, K2, SB3, K2, SB1, K2
Rows 23 - 24	SL1, K1, SB1, K2, SB4, K2, SB1, K2, SB4, K2, SB1, K2
Rows 25 - 26	SL1, K1, SB1, K2, SB5, K2, SB1, K2, SB5, K2, SB1, K2
Rows 27 - 28**	SL1, K1, SB1, K2, SB6, K2, SB1, K2, SB6, K2, SB1, K2
Rows 29 - 30	SL1, K1, SB2, K2, SB5, K2, SB2, K2, SB5, K2, SB2, K2
Rows 31 - 32	SL1, K1, SB3, K2, SB4, K2, SB3, K2, SB4, K2, SB3, K2
Rows 33 - 34	SL1, K1, SB4, K2, SB3, K2, SB4, K2, SB3, K2, SB4, K2
Rows 35 - 36	SL1, K1, SB5, K2, SB2, K2, SB5, K2, SB2, K2, SB5, K2
Rows 37 - 38	SL1, K1, SB6, K2, SB1, K2, SB6, K2, SB1, K2, SB6, K2
Rows 39 - 40	SL1, K1, SB5, K2, SB2, K2, SB5, K2, SB2, K2, SB5, K2
Rows 41 - 42	SL1, K1, SB4, K2, SB3, K2, SB4, K2, SB3, K2, SB4, K2
Rows 43 - 44	SL1, K1, SB3, K2, SB4, K2, SB3, K2, SB4, K2, SB3, K2
Rows 45 - 46	SL1, K1, SB2, K2, SB5, K2, SB2, K2, SB5, K2, SB2, K2**

Repeat pattern from ** to ** three times to complete Rows 47 - 106

Rows 107 - 108	SL1, K1, SB1, K2, SB6, K2, SB1, K2, SB6, K2, SB1, K2
Rows 109 - 110	SL1, K1, SB1, K2, SB5, K2, SB1, K2, SB5, K2, SB1, K2
Rows 111 - 112	SL1, K1, SB1, K2, SB4, K2, SB1, K2, SB4, K2, SB1, K2
Rows 113 - 114	SL1, K1, SB1, K2, SB3, K2, SB1, K2, SB3, K2, SB1, K2
Rows 115 - 116	SL1, K1, SB1, K2, SB2, K2, SB1, K2, SB2, K2, SB1, K2
Rows 117 - 118	SL1, K1, SB1, K2, SB1, K2, SB1, K2, SB1, K2, SB1, K2
Rows 119 - 130	Knit across and bind off

Attach the Clasp

To attach clasp, fold end of bracelet over the clasp and stitch into place using the big eye needle.

Braided Ndebele Cuff

Supplies:

- 11° seed beads ≈15g
- 11° triangle beads ≈40g
- Thread
- Size 10 beading needle

The braided bangle is made from three flat woven strips using triangle beads and seed beads.

N°45

Beginning the Bracelet

String on an 11, three triangles, and 11, three triangles. Go back through the next to the last triangle bead in the same direction that the needle went through it in the first place.

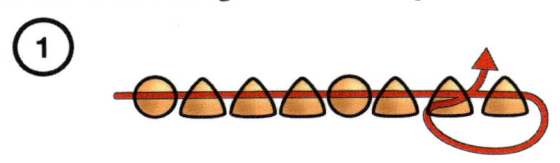

①

Go back through the next triangle bead.

②

Continue in this manner until you have completed the ladder. Join the ladder into a circle by going back through the last triangle bead. Note the position of the triangle beads.

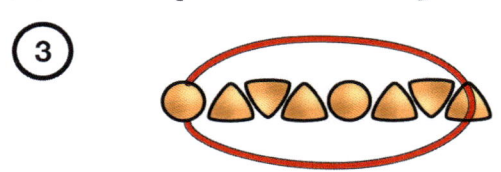

③

The following diagram shows what the circle of beads will look like when viewed from above. It is important to maintain the position of the triangle beads through the tubular ndebele.

④

Begin tubular ndebele (herringbone stitch) as follows. With the thread exiting a size 11 seed bead, pick up an 11 and a triangle and go down through the triangle bead in the ladder that is to the left of the bead your thread is exiting. Pass the needle back up through the next triangle bead.

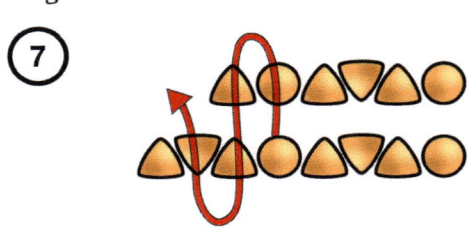

⑤

Pick up two triangle beads and go down through the next triangle bead. Pass the thread back up through the size 11 seed bead.

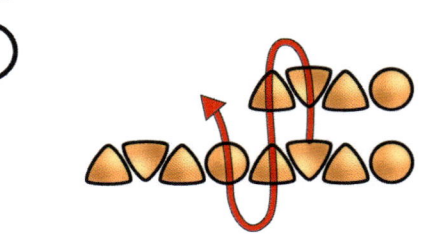

⑥

Pick up an 11 and a triangle and go down through the triangle bead in the ladder that is to the left of the bead your thread is exiting. Pass the needle back up through the next triangle bead.

⑦

Pick up two triangle beads and go down through the next triangle bead. Pass the thread back up through two size 11 seed beads to make the step up.

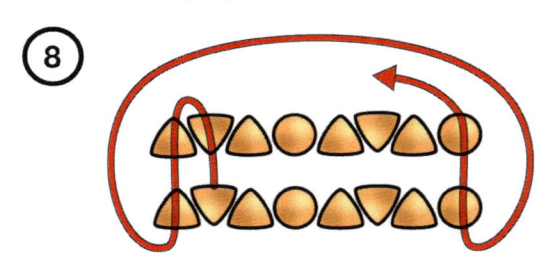

⑧

Continue tubular ndebele (*i.e. herringbone*) until the piece measures one inch longer than the fattest part of your hand. The table below shows some measurements for various finished size bracelets.

7" finished length:	8" strip
8" finished length:	9 1/8" strip
9" finished length:	10 1/4" strip

You will need to make three strips in the correct length.

Tack the three strips together at the end to hold in place while braiding. Lay the three strips side by side and sew the end of each strip to the other strips.

Beginning the Bracelet

9 Tack the ends of the strips together.

These tacking threads will be removed later so make the stitches large and visible. You may wish to use a contrast color thread to make the tack stitches easy to identify.

Braid the three strips loosely and tack the strips together at the other end just as you did at the first end. Make sure that each strip lines up with the beginning of the same strip.

In other words, connect the end of the yellow strip to the opposite end of the yellow strip, the end of the light brown strip to the opposite end of the light brown strip and the end of the dark brown strip to the opposite end of the dark brown strip.

Connect the ends of the tubular ndebele by stitching back and forth through the beads around the tubes. Keep each tube separate from the next one.

Take out the tack stitches & congratulations on your new bracelet.

Nº 47

Russian Leaf Earrings

Supplies:

- Delica beads DB 042 ≈3g
- Delica beads DB 041≈1g
- Size 10 beading needle
- Nymo Thread Size D
- Earring findings of your choice

These delicate earrings are stitched in a Russian Leaf pattern in silver with gold edging. Very classy earrings and easy to stitch.

Nº 48

Beginning the Leaf

Begin at the tip of the leaf and string on 1 gold bead to the center of about a yard of conditioned beading thread. The second side will be stitched with the remaining thread. String on 7 silver beads, one gold bead and 1 silver bead. Go back through the 6th silver bead strung. (*See Diagram 1.*)

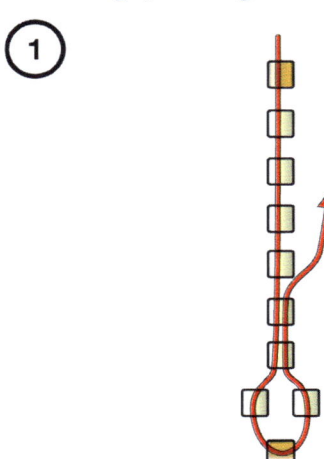

1

String one silver bead, skip a bead in the first row and go through the next bead. Stitch three peyote stitches exiting through the gold bead. (*See diagram 2.*) See the resource section for basic peyote stitch.

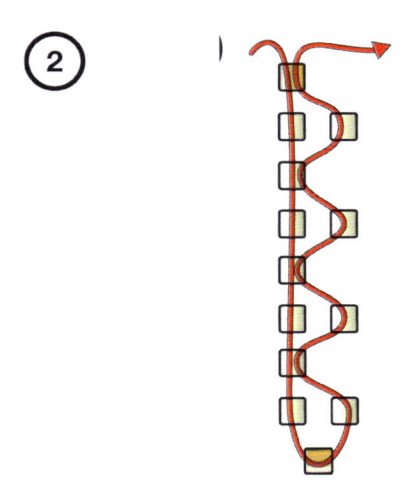

2

Turn the work and string on one silver bead go back through the last silver bead added and then make two peyote stitches in silver beads. Add a picot at the bottom by adding a gold bead and a silver bead. And going back through the previous silver bead added. (*See Diagram 3.*)

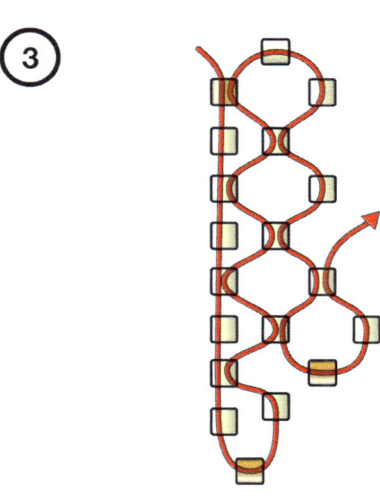

3

Continue back up with peyote and at the top of the row. Add one gold bead and one silver bead and continue to peyote back to the bottom of the row. (*See Diagram 4.*)

To make the decrease at the bottom of the row, peyote until you reach the next to the last bead in the row, then add one gold and one silver and go back through the next bead for peyote stitch. (*See Diagram 4.*)

To rest of the increases at the top are made by adding two silver, one gold and one silver bead. Go back through the first bead added (silver) and then continue peyote down the row. (*See Diagram 4.*)

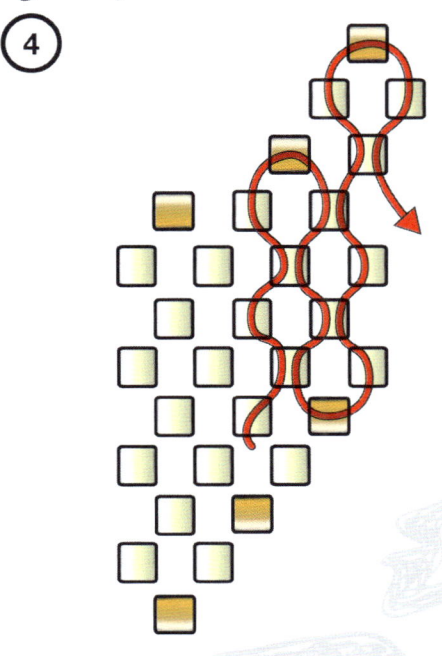

4

N° 49

Continue making increases at the top, and decreases at the bottom until you have six gold beads on the inside of the leaf, not counting the center gold bead. Repeat the same for the other side of the leaf. (*See Diagram 5.*)

Join the Top of the Leaves

When you have completed the required number of increases and decreases, join the top of the small leaf together as follows:

With thread exiting the last bead added, string on two silver beads and connect to the same bead as the last bead added on the other side of the leaf. Come back up through the bead next to it, pick up two silver beads and go through the same bead on the other side of the leaf. Weave the thread to the center of the top of the leaf. (See diagram 5.)

Add a loop for hanging using five silver beads. Do not end the thread – it will be used to stitch the inside veins of the leaves. Stitch a second leaf using the same process until there are seven gold beads on the inside of the leaf not including the center gold bead. Do not join the top of this leaf. Attach the larger leaf to the smaller leaf at the location marked on the chart.

Embellish the Leaves With Veins

With the thread from the top of the first leaf, stitch veins in the centers of the leaves as follows: Make the center vein by picking up enough beads to reach from the top of the leaf to the bottom. Weave through the bottom of the top leaf and do the same for the bottom leaf. Then weave the thread back up the inner sides of the leaf to add the side veins. This is where you can be creative. You can follow the picture provided or place the veins in the way that you like best.

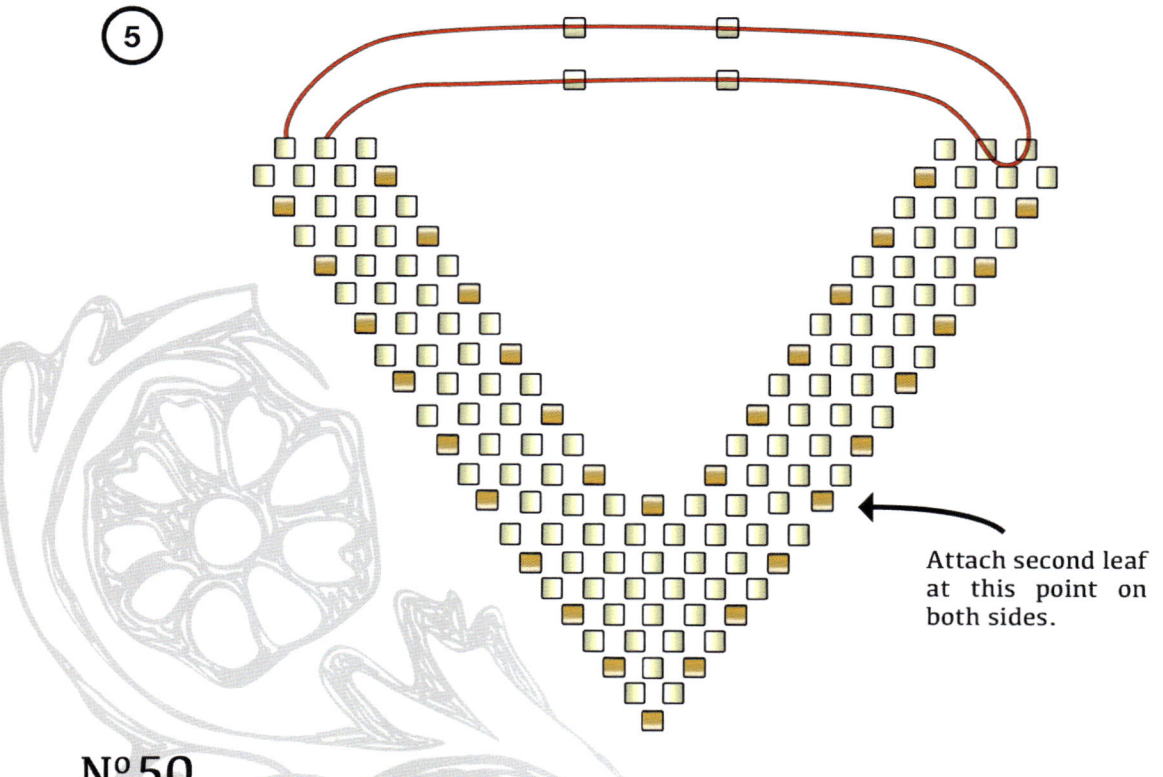

⑤

Attach second leaf at this point on both sides.

Nº 50

N°51

Framed Peyote Earrings

Supplies:

- 11° seed beads ≈5g
- 46 4mm gold filled beads
- 2 Earring findings
- Nymo Thread Size D (*to match the beads as closely as possible*)
- Beading needles size 12

This great looking pair of earrings is made using a frame of seed beads and a peyote weaving using gold filled beads.

N° 52

Ladder Stitch

Begin with a 5' length of Nymo thread, stretch it well and use wax or thread heaven if desired. Leave an 8" tail and string on 4 delica beads and go back through the first two beads again from the bottom. (*See Diagram 1.*) See the resource section for basics on the ladder stitch.

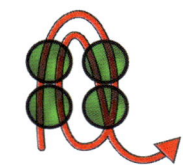

①

Pick up two more beads and go back through the last two beads of your ladder. (*See Diagram 2.*) Then go through the last two beads added.

Pick up two more beads. Then go back through the two beads previously added.

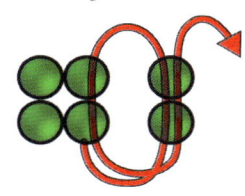

②

Continue to add stacks of two beads until you have 14 stacks across.

Square Stitch

Add a third row of beads using square stitch. (*See Diagram 3.*) See the resource section for basics on the square stitch.

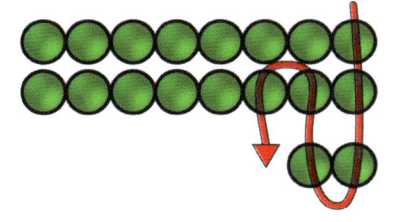

③

Add two beads for the first stitch and go back through the second bead in the previous row. From this point add one bead each time and pass the needle back through the previous bead added and the bead in the row below. Come up through the bead next to it and back up through the beads just added. (*See diagram 4.*)

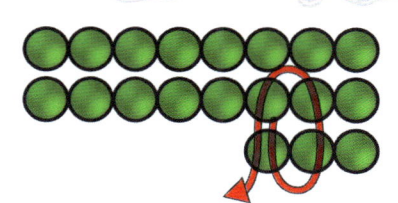

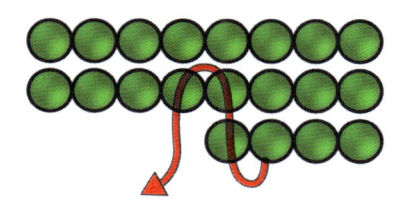

④

When the fourth row gets started, only add three beads. Work the three beads for eleven rows.

Weave the needle back down to the other side of the original three bead base rows and work eleven rows of three beads on that side. At this point you will have three sides of the frame complete.

Work ladder stitch again for eight beads to form the connection for the fourth side. Work two more rows of square stitch to complete the frame.

Add the Inside Design

Weave the needle so that it is coming out of the second stack of eight beads between the two sides. (*See Diagram 5.*)

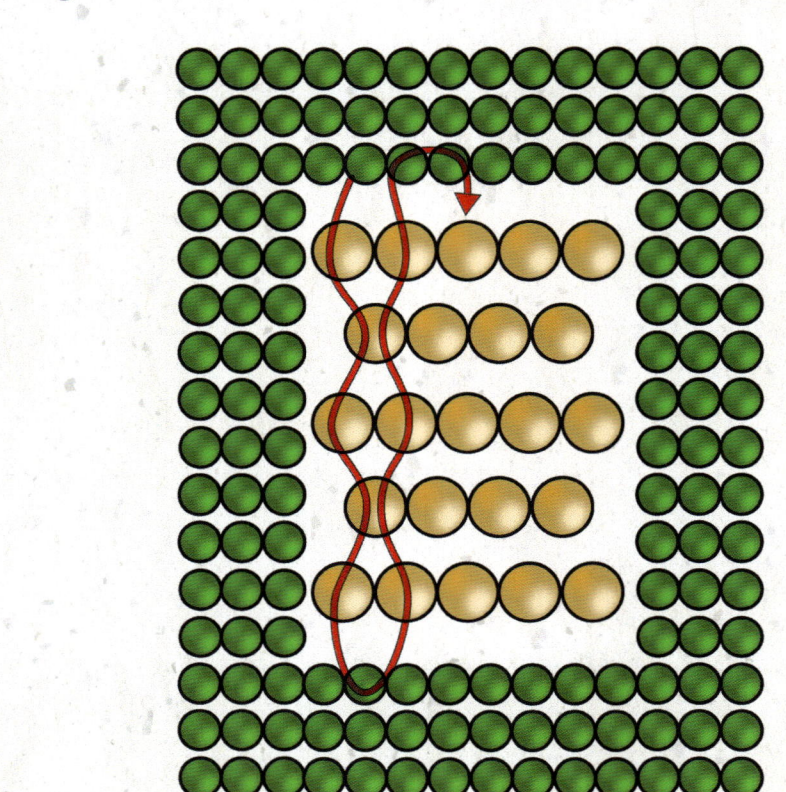

⑤

String on five gold filled balls and go through the matching bead in the bottom part of the frame. Thread the needle over to the next bead and pick up one gold bead to begin the peyote stitch. Continue peyote across the opening in the frame as shown in diagram 5.

Attach the Earring Findings

Weave the needle over to one of the corners and make a 7 bead loop. Go back through the loop again to reinforce. Attach the earring finding of your choice to the loop. Make sure you choose the same corner of the second earring to attaché the loop so that the earrings will match.

Winter Snowflake Earrings

Supplies:

- 120 2.5 mm bi-cone Swarovski Crystals AB
- 15° seed beads in gold (less than 1 gram)
- Crystal Fireline
- Size 10 or 11 needles

Create these fabulous snowflake earrings with circular triangle weave.

N° 55

Starting the Flake

Thread a needle with about 1-½ yards of thread or Fireline. String on a 15° seed bead, a 2.5 mm crystal, a 15° seed bead, a 2.5 mm crystal, a 15° seed bead and a 2.5 mm crystal. Tie beads into a circle.

(1)

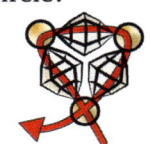

Weave the thread so that it is exiting one of the crystals. String on a seed bead, a crystal, a seed bead, a crystal and a seed bead. Go back through the crystal that the thread is coming out of. You will be going in a circle.

(2)

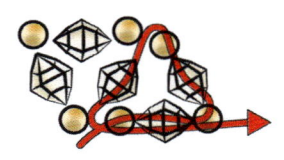

Weave the thread so that it is exiting one of the crystals. String on a seed bead, a crystal, a seed bead, a crystal and a seed bead. Go back through the crystal that the thread is coming out of. You will be going in a circle. Notice that this time you will be going in the opposite direction.

(3)

Weave the thread so that it is exiting a crystal spoke bead of the circle as shown. String on a seed bead, a crystal, a seed bead, a crystal and a seed bead. Go back through the crystal that the thread is coming out of. You will be going in a circle.

(4)

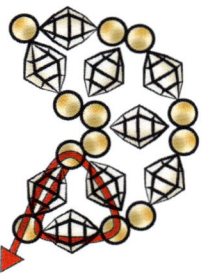

Weave the thread so that it is exiting a crystal spoke bead of the circle as shown. String on a seed bead, a crystal, a seed bead, a crystal and a seed bead. Go back through the crystal that the thread is coming out of. You will be going in a circle. Notice that this time you will be going in the opposite direction.

(5)

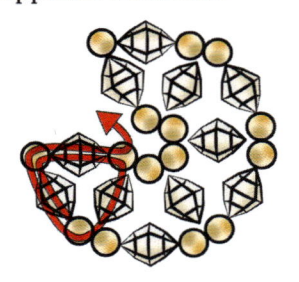

To complete the circle, pick up a seed bead and connect to the beginning crystal. Then pick up a seed bead, a crystal, and a seed bead. Go through the end completing the circle/wheel shape as shown. Weave the thread back to the center of the heart and go through the circle of seeds at the center to pull them tight.

(6)

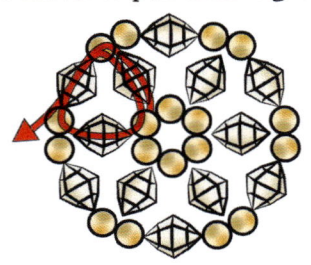

Weave your thread so that it is exiting the circle as shown.

(7)

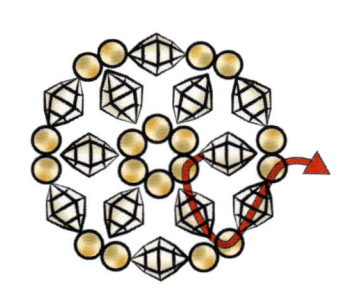

Nº 56

Pick up one seed bead, one crystal, one seed bead, one crystal and one seed bead. Go back through the crystal that the thread is coming out of. Weave back through the beads just added until the thread is coming out of the first crystal added and the following seed bead.

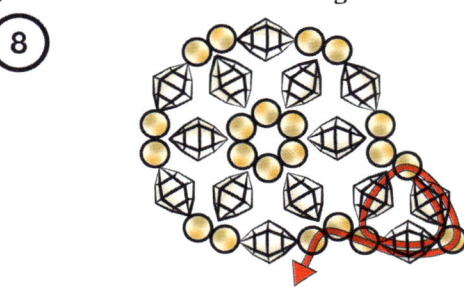

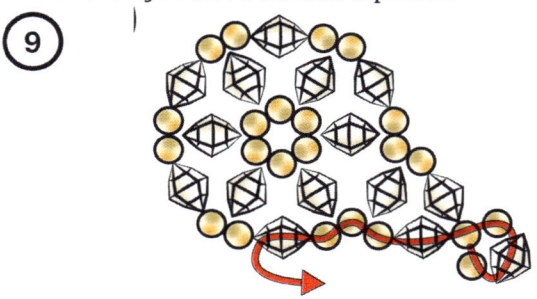

⑧

Pick up one seed bead, one crystal, one seed bead, and weave back through the bead added in the last step as shown in the diagram. This will form the point of the icicle. Continue steps 8 and 9 until you have formed 6 points.

⑨

Pick up one seed bead, one crystal, one seed bead, and weave back through the bead added in the last step as shown in the diagram. This will form the point of the icicle. Continue steps 8 and 9 until you have formed 6 points.

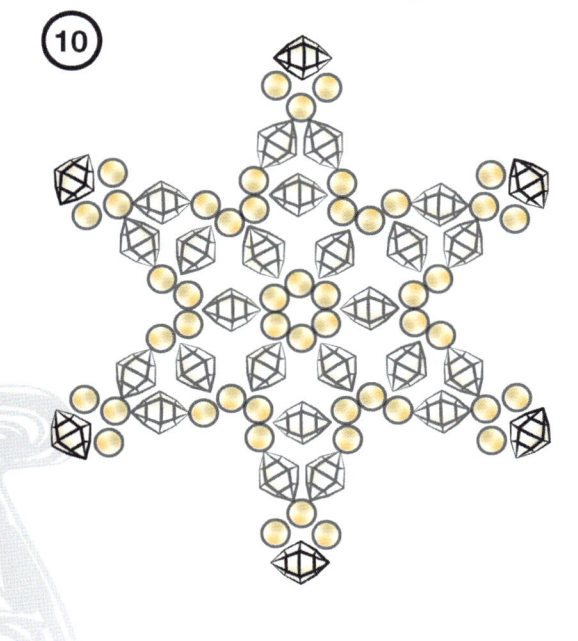

⑩

You be adding a crystal between each point to add strength to the snowflake. Repeat around using the 15° seed beads on one side then switch to the other side and using the same crystal, connect between the 15° beads on the second side as shown in the diagram.

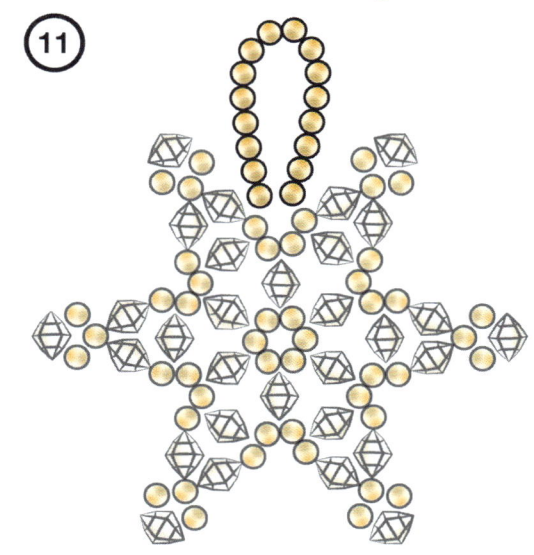

⑪

Add a loop to the crystal at one of the points using 15° seed beads in order to create a bail. We used 7 seed beads and went back through them several times to create strength at the stress point. The earrings measure about 1" across in diameter.

If you wanted to make a pendant, you could use 3 mm or 4 mm crystals and 15° or 11° seed beads to make a larger version for a pendant.

Twisted Ribbon Necklace

Supplies:

- 11° delica beads (gold lined crystal) ≈ 4g
- 4lb Fireline
- 1.5 mm cube beads in 3 colors (40 g {blue, green, purple} each)
- size 10 or 11 needles

Use cubes and delicas to create a beautiful 3D ribbon effect.

Nº 58

Begin the Loops

Thread a length of Fireline with one needle. Use a length that is comfortable for you to stitch with. Waxing the Fireline will reduce knots. String on one gold delica, one blue cube, one delica, one purple cube, one delica, one green cube, one delica, one green cube, one delica, one purple cube, one delica and one blue cube.

①

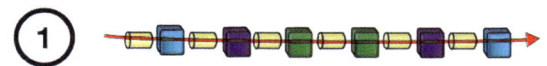

Stitch a ladder stitch, following the diagram. Skip the last bead and go through the next to the last bead in the same direction as before, then each subsequent bead in the same direction. The beads will line up next to each other.

②

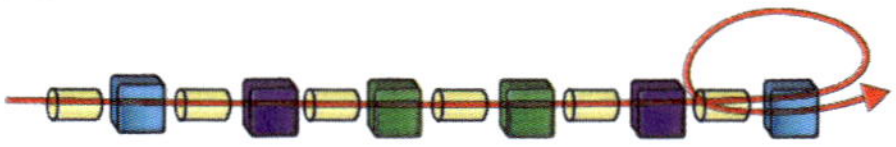

The beads will line up next to each other with the holes pointing up.

③

Connect the line of beads into a circle.

④

Begin herringbone stitch as follows. With the thread exiting the blue cube bead, pick up a gold delica and a blue cube bead. Go down through the gold delica and come back up through the purple cube.

⑤

Next pick up a gold delica, and a purple cube. Go back down through the gold delica and back up through the green cube.

⑥

Next pick up a gold delica, and a purple cube. Go back down through the gold delica and back up through the green cube.

⑦

Continue in the same manner on the back side. You will need to step up through the blue cube and the gold bead in the front when you finish the back. You will always step up at this point as you add additional rows. When you add additional rows, make sure to alternate the cubes and delicas to create the ribbon pattern.

Each link will need to be 68 rows long. When this length is attained, twist the strip one full twist and connect the ends together. Make the connections by going through a few beads on each side of the join, then crossing to the opposite side and going through a few beads. You may need to flip the loop as you are joining the ends together.

When you get the second strip complete, make sure that you twist in the same direction and put one end through the previous loop before joining the ends. Make as many loops as you need for the desired length. We used 17 loops in our sample. This is large enough to allow the necklace to slip over the head.

When you make the last join, twist the loop once, then pass the end through the first loop and the previous loop. Make sure the twist is in the correct direction so that the pattern matches from beginning to end. This might take a few tries to get it right (*at least it did for me!*). Enjoy your new necklace.

Fun with Faux Pearls

Supplies:

- 2mm plastic pearls round ≈ 340
- 3mm plastic pearls round ≈ 340
- Rice shaped plastic pearls ≈ 340
- 10 mm beads ≈ 17
- Nymo thread
- Microcrystalline wax
- Size 12 beading needle

Have fun with plastic "pearls" to make this interesting necklace with beaded beads.

N° 60

Making the Spheres

Use about 3 yards of thread, doubled, heavily waxed for this project.

String on one 2mm, one rice, one 3mm, one rice and one 2mm sequence of beads. Follow the thread path closely. Go back through the second rice, the 3mm and the first rice. Pass the needle through the first 2mm bead in the same direction as it went through the bead originally.

1

String on the same sequence again and repeat the same thread path. Snug the sequence up close to the first sequence.

2

Continue until you have 9 bead sequences. They will be starting to form a circle at this point. You will be joining them into a circle by connecting the first 2mm bead with the last 2mm bead as shown in the diagram.

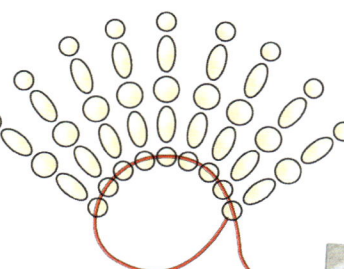

3

Weave your needle through to the other end of the spokes and connect all the outside 2mm beads into a circle. Go through the beads again to make a very tight circle.

Weave your needle though one of the spokes until you reach a 3mm bead. You will be placing additional three mm beads between the beads in the spoke, both on top and underneath. When you have completed one time around continue around again placing beads above or below depending on where they were placed the first time. Tension is very important here since the peyote beaded rows in the center of the bead give it the strength to maintain the round shape.

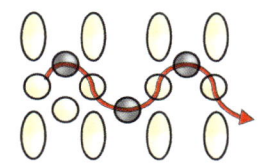

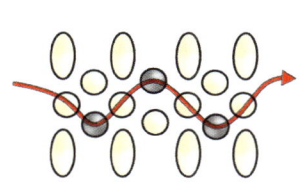

4

5

When you have completed the second pass, weave in your threads. You have now completed your first pearl bead. Stitch as many beads as you need to reach the length you want. You can combine the pearl beads with many different beads to create new looks.

Peyote Spiral Necklace

Supplies:

- Size 6 seed beads ≈ 9g
- Size 8 seed beads (*two colors*) ≈ 11g
- Size 11 seed beads (*two colors*) ≈ 10g
- 315 Size 15 seed beads (*two colors*) ≈ 6g
- Size 12 beading needle
- Clasp + 2 colored jump rings

Keep tight tension throughout this project for best results. Heavily waxing the thread will help.

N° 62

Stitching the Swirls

String on a stop bead and leave about a 6 inch tail.

Then string the beads as follows:

- 2 – 6°
- 2 – 8° color A
- 2 – 8° color B
- 2 – 11° color A
- 2 – 11° color B
- 2 – 15° color A
- 2 – 15° color A
- 2 – 15° dolor A
- 2 – 11° color B
- 2 – 11° color A
- 2 – 8° color B
- 2 – 8° color A

Form a circle by passing the needle through the two size 6° beads and tying a knot. Make sure that your needle is coming out of the 2nd 6° bead. Begin peyote stitch by picking up the same bead as the bead size and color that the thread is exiting. At the end of the round, you will need to step up. Continue in this pattern until the desired length of swirls is complete.

Decreasing for the Neckband

Begin decreasing every few rows by stitching through two beads without adding a bead. The goal is to end up with only the 2 size 11° colors to continue the neckband. So for the first decrease, stitch through the two 8°'s and on the opposite side of the round stitch through the two 8°'s. Stitch a couple of rows with no decrease. Second decrease, stitch through the 6° and the 8° and then stitch through two 15°'s. Stitch a couple of rows with no decrease. Continue in this manner until you have only the size 11° beads remaining. Continue in the spiral peyote stitch until the neckband is the desired length. Repeat these steps on the other end of the necklace.

Attach the Clasp

Attach the clasp to the neckband by stitching repeatedly through the clasp and through the beads in the neckband until a good firm connection is achieved. Enjoy your beautiful spiral necklace.

Nº 63

La Côte Azure

Supplies:

- 4mm round crystals clear AB ≈ 9
- 4mm round crystals emerald ≈ 60
- 4mm round crystal siam ≈ 60
- 4mm round crystals sapphire ≈ 29
- 8 size 12mm round rivolis sapphire ≈ 8
- 2mm round crystals clear AB ≈ 174
- 11° seed beads galvanized gold ≈ 3g
- 15° seed beads galvanized gold ≈ 12g
- Size 11 or 12 needles
- Clear Fireline 4lb

This gorgeous necklace utilizes several sizes of crystals to add sparkle and shine to the piece.

Bezeling the Rivoli

String on 16 beads size 15° and tie into a circle.

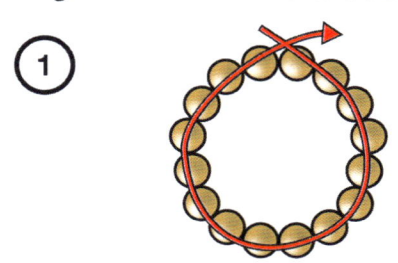

1

Make five bead picots eight times by stringing on 5 beads, skipping the next bead in the circle and go through the next bead.

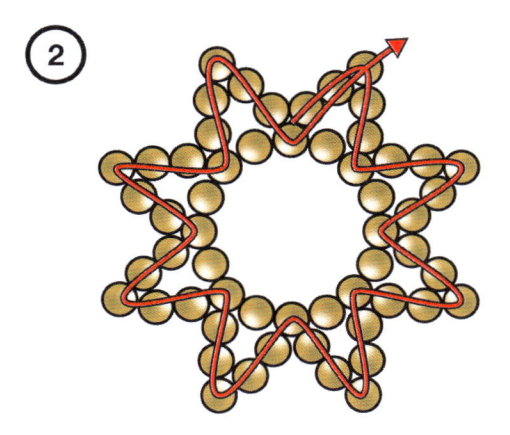

2

Weave the needle until it is coming out of the center bead of the 5 bead picot. String on three beads and go into the middle bead of the next 5 bead picot. Continue around.

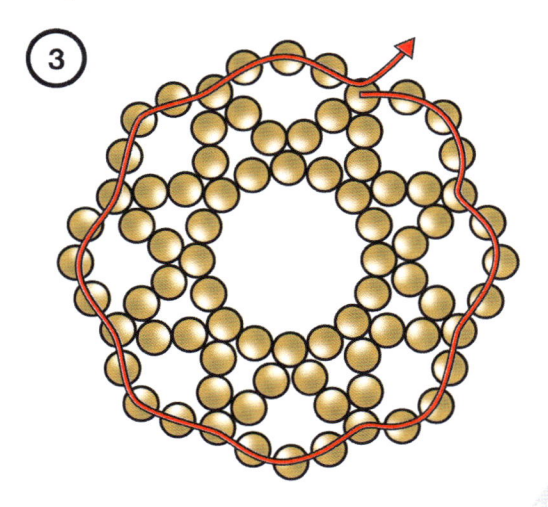

3

Treat the three beads from the last round as one unit and place one 11° bead in between each of the three bead units.

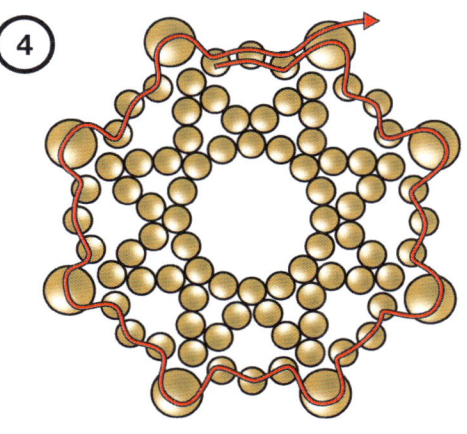

4

Weave the needle so that it is coming out of one of the 11° beads. String on three beads between each of the 11° beads.

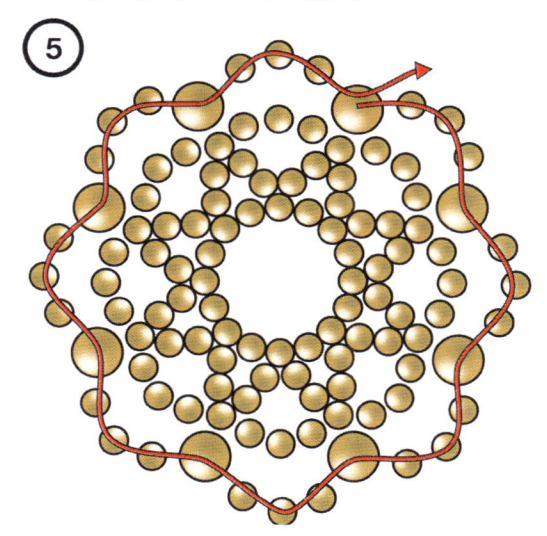

5

N°65

Weave the needle so that it is coming out of the middle bead of the three beads added in the last round. String on three beads and go through the center bead of the next three beads. Insert the rivoli before finishing this round.

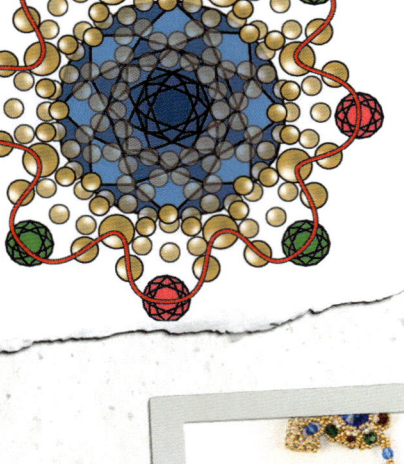

Weave the needle so that it is coming out of the 15° bead next to the crystal. Add eight 15° beads to circle the crystal and go through the 15° bead on the other side of the crystal.

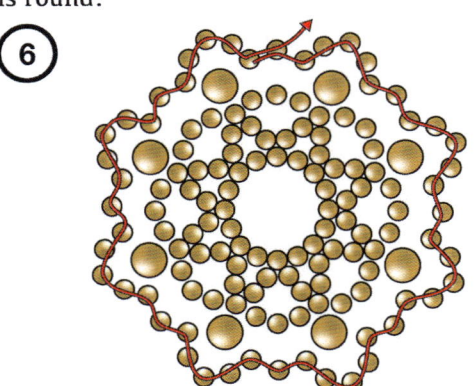

Weave the needle back to one of the 11° beads. String on one 15°, one 4 mm red crystal, and one 15°. Make sure you alternate the red and green crystals around the edge of the rivoli bezel.

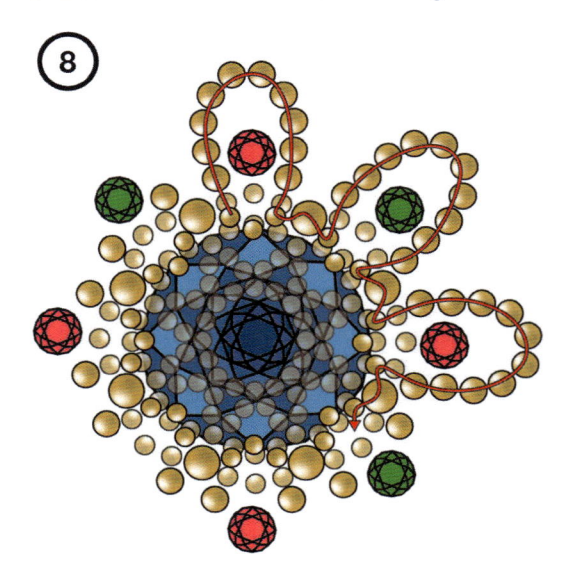

Go through two of the 15° beads between the crystals and add one 11° bead. Go through the two 15° beads on the side of the next crystal.

Weave needle back to edge of bezel and add 2mm crystals in between the next to the last round and the last round of the bezeling on the front on the rivoli.

N°66

Making the Right Angle Weave Units

Cubic Right Angle Weave (*CRAW*) for three units make 90° turn and add two more units.

Embellish with 2mm crystals.

Pick up four beads and tie them into a circle. Think of this as the bottom on a box. Go through one more bead.

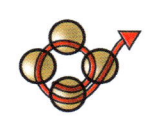

⑨

Pick up 2 beads and go through the closest wall bead and the bead that the thread was coming out of in the bottom of the box. Go through the next bottom bead. You have now made the second wall of the box.

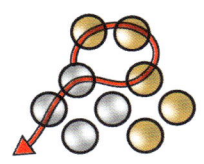

⑪

Repeat the previous step to construct the third wall of the box. Note that in this picture the bottom of the box is shown in gray.

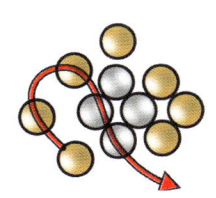

⑫

For the fourth side of the box, go through the wall bead of the first side of the box, pick up one bead, go through the wall bead of the third side of the box, then through the bottom bead the thread is coming out of. Note the bottom bead is shown in dark gray and the side beads are shown in light gray.

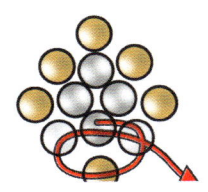

⑬

Now weave up to the four top beads of the box. Go through them securing the top of the box. This now becomes the bottom of the box for you to construct another 2 Boxes.

Weave your needle so that you are coming out of the side of the last box. You will proceed with tubular CRAW at a 90° angle for two boxes.

The 2mm crystals are attached in the middle of each box by weaving the Fireline as shown in the diagram. Weave the Fireline in, make some half hitch knots and then weave through a few more beads and cut the Fireline.

Make 23 CRAW units that are three boxes long with three boxes at a right angle. Make one RAW unit for the center piece that is four boxes long with three boxes at a right angle.

Making the Crystal Units

String on a red crystal, 15°, green crystal, 15°, crystal, 15°, green crystal, 15°. Tie into a circle.

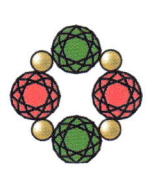

⑭

Make an X on the face of the circle by adding 5 beads and crossing to the opposite 15°, weave through the crystal and come out of the 15°. Add two 15° beads, then go through the middle bead of the 5 added in the last step and add two more beads before going through the 15° opposite.

⑮

Making the Center Piece

With the needle coming out of one of the 11° beads between the red and green crystals on a rivoli unit, string on 5 size 15° gold seed beads, one 4mm sapphire crystal, and five more 15° gold seed beads. Go back through the 11° bead in the rivoli unit. Weave your thread back through the path until it is coming out of the 4 mm sapphire crystal.

Attach the sides of one CRAW unit to the 4mm sapphire crystal by connecting to one of the 11° beads closest to the center on the end of the CRAW unit.

Weave your needle down to the bottom of the CRAW unit and string on four 15° gold seed beads, one 4mm crystal ab, and 4 15° gold seed beads. Weave back through the bottom of the CRAW and follow the path back down so that the thread is coming out of the ab crystal. String on one 15° seed bead, one 4mm crystal ab, one 15° seed beads, on 4mm crystal and one 15° seed bead. Weave back through the original crystal and go around the three crystals and seed beads a few times to reinforce.

Weave the thread so that it is coming out of the seed bead in-between the two crystal ab beads at the bottom of the unit.

String on three 15° seed beads, go through the 11° bead in between a rivoli unit red and green crystals. String on three more 15° seed beads and follow the path to reinforce.

Weave you thread to the opposite side of the rivoli unit and with the needle coming out of the 11° seed bead string on four 15° seed beads, one sapphire crystal and four 15° seed beads. Follow the path back down to the sapphire crystal and go through it. Attach the four unit CRAW unit to the sapphire crystal in the same way as described above.

Make two units using a crystal unit, a CRAW unit, three crystal ab beads and seed beads as described above for the main unit, a rivoli unit and a CRAW unit.

Use the same methods as described for the center piece to construct the rest of the pieces.

Second Unit

Make two of these units.

Third and Fifth Unit

Make four of these units.

Small Unit

Create ten of these units or as many as you need to fit your neck.

Connecting the Units

Connect one unit to another by exiting the center piece through the 11° bead that is one to the right or left from the center top. String on three 15° beads, one 4mm sapphire and three 15° beads. Go through the 15° bead beside the emerald crystal at the top of the second unit and string on three more 15°, go through the sapphire crystal and back through the 11° bead in the rivoli. Each piece is connected in the same manner.

After the last piece is connected you may want to vary the number of 15° seed beads before and after the sapphire crystal when you are attaching the clasp. You can add or subtract 15°s to make the fit that you want.

Resources Section

Flat Peyote Stitch Even Count

It is helpful to use two colors of beads while you are learning. String on alternating colors so that you have an even number of beads. I am using six beads in the diagrams. Then pick up a grey bead, skip over the last grey bead and go through the white bead. You will be actually stitching the third row. The first beads that were strung on make up the first and second rows. This becomes more obvious after the third row is complete.

At the end of the third row you will turn around and head back in the other direction. Pick up a white bead and go through the next grey bead. You will only be adding white beads on this row.

For the next row repeat with grey beads going back in the other direction.

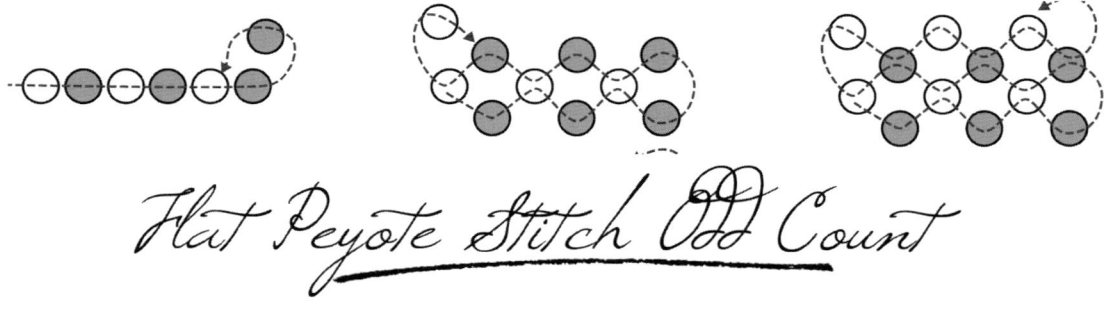

Flat Peyote Stitch Odd Count

This is the catch the loop below method for Encrusted Jewels.

For the first row catch the tail thread and come back through the last bead.

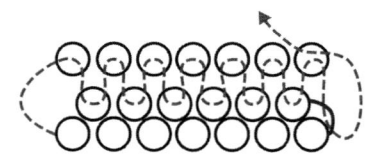

For the next row, catch the thread loop from the row below.

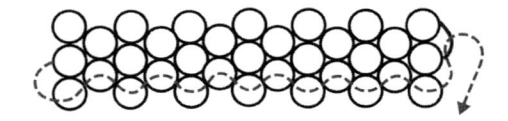

Nº 70

Flat Peyote Stitch Odd Count Step up Method

Tubular Peyote Stitch

Pick up an even number of beads and tie them into a circle. Pick up 1 bead, skip one bead in the circle and go through the next bead of the circle. Pick up 1 bead, skip the next bead in the circle and go through the next bead in the circle. Continue in this manner until you have added one-half the number of beads in the beginning circle. In order to step-up, go through the first bead added in the second round in order to be in the correct position to start the next round. You will need to step up at the end of each round.

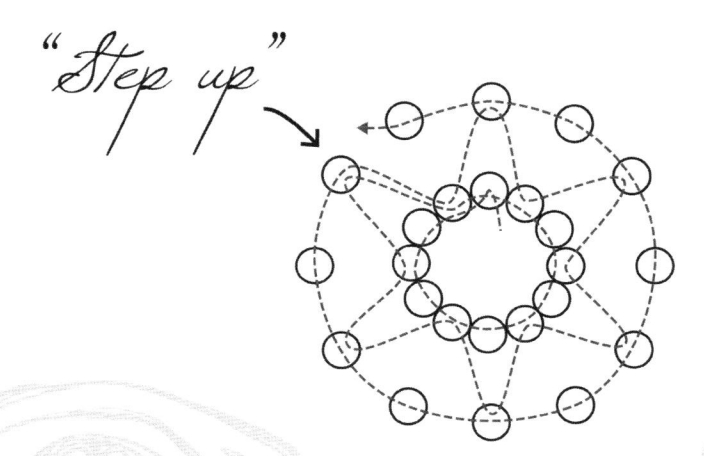

"Step up"

Cubic Right Angle Weave (CRAW)

Pick up four beads and tie them into a circle. Think of this as the bottom on a box. Go through one more bead.

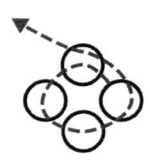

Pick up 3 beads. Pass the thread back through the bead that the thread is coming out of making a circle. This will make the first side of the box. Go through the next bead in the "bottom" of the box.

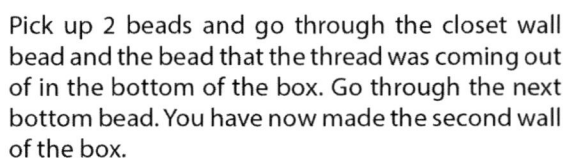

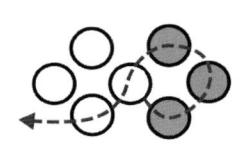

Pick up 2 beads and go through the closet wall bead and the bead that the thread was coming out of in the bottom of the box. Go through the next bottom bead. You have now made the second wall of the box.

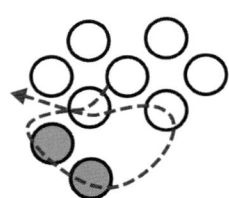

Repeat the previous step to construct the third wall of the box.

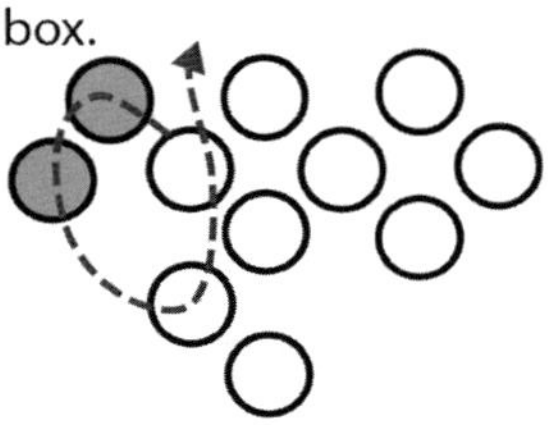

For the fourth side of the box, go through the wall bead of the first side of the box, pick up one bead, go through the wall bead on the third side of the box, then through the bottom bead the thread is coming out of.

Surgeon's Knot

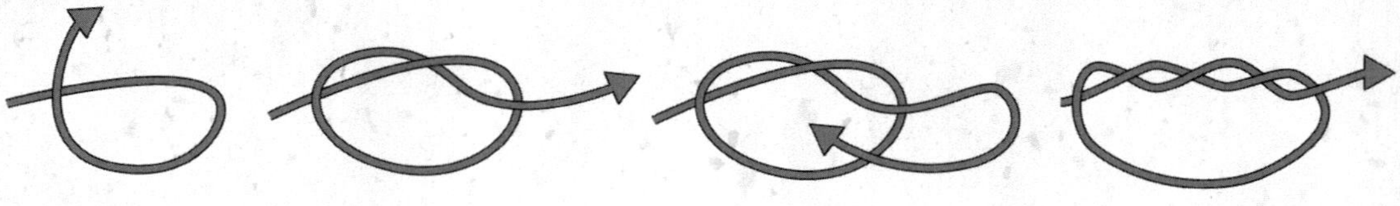

Herringbone Stitch

This is an alternative method of starting the stitch without using a ladder stitch to begin. Start by picking up twelve beads. The first bead will be white and then you will follow the pattern of alternating double grey and double white. At the end of the twelve though you will end on one white just like you began.

To begin the stitch add a bead to make the turn, in this case I used a grey bead. Coming out of the white bead string on the grey bead and pass back through the white bead. You will then skip the next two grey beads and pass through the other next white bead.

You will then add on two more grey beads and pass through the next white bead. This stitch will create an interesting appearance, that is emphasized more when using tubular shaped beads. Repeat these steps all the way down the row.

To turn add on one grey bead and a white bead and pass back through the grey bead that you just added and then skip the next two white beads passing back through the next grey bead. Continue to use this method until you have reached your desired length. Tie off and bury the thread. The only difference between flat herringbone and tubular is that in tubular you are working in a complete circle.

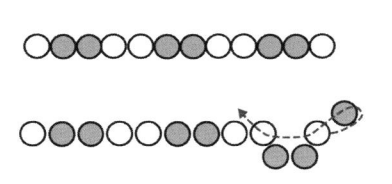

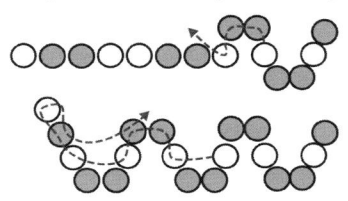

Square Knot

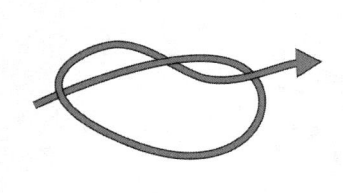

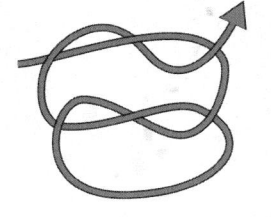

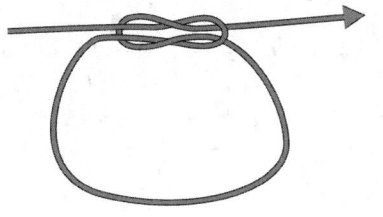

Ladder Stitch

Pick up the number of beads required for the first row of the ladder. Go back through the beads according to the diagram for the first row. Each row lines up with the previous row. Ladder stitch is often used as a base for herringbone stitch.

Brick Stitch

Begin each row with two beads. Catch the second loop and go back up through the first beads and down through the second bead. Catch the loop again and go up through the second bead.

For the rest of the row, pick up one bead, go under the next thread loop, and back up through the bead. Continue across the row.

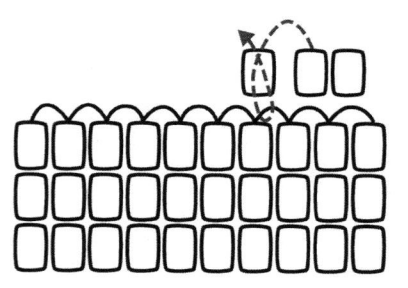

Elizabeth Townes
BeadJewled, Inc.
www.beadjeweledinc.com

Printed in Great Britain
by Amazon